The Vardon Invasion

Harry's Triumphant 1900
American Tour

Bob Labbance
with Brian Siplo

Foreword by Tony Jacklin

SPORTS
MEDIA
GROUP®

All inquiries should be addressed to:
Sports Media Group
An imprint of Ann Arbor Media Group
2500 S. State Street
Ann Arbor, MI 48104

Printed in the United States of America.

1 2 3 4 5

ISBN 13: 978-1-58726-294-4
ISBN 10: 1-58726-294-0

Library of Congress Cataloging in Publication data

Labbance, Bob.
  The Vardon invasion : Harry's triumphant 1900 American tour / Bob Labbance with Brian Siplo ; foreword by Tony Jacklin.
      p. cm.
  Includes bibliographical references and index.
  ISBN-13: 978-1-58726-294-4 (hardcover : alk. paper)
  ISBN-10: 1-58726-294-0 (hardcover : alk. paper)
  1. Vardon, Harry,
1870-1937. 2. Golfers--England. 3. Golf--United States--History. I. Siplo,
Brian. II. Title.

GV964.V3.L33 2008
796.352092--dc22
[B]
                                                                2007047506

Contents

Foreword

Growing up in Scunthorpe, England in the 1940s and 1950s it would have been natural for me to pursue football or cricket. I played some football, but injuries were a concern and I found cricket a complete bore. So, during the summer of my ninth year, I began caddieing for my father at Scunthorpe Golf Club. After he had played he would give me an old cut-down ladies 3-wood to hit, and so I became hooked on the game.

I first became aware of Harry Vardon as a young man. Although he had passed away in 1937, Vardon's legacy set a standard for all English golf professionals to follow. Not only had he established a playing record that future golf accomplishments would forever be compared with, he emerged from a humble background to conduct himself with class and dignity on the world stage—a standard for all of us to emulate.

In 1973, I moved to Jersey and lived there for eight years and Vardon's presence still loomed large on the island. My oldest daughter Tina was born there and I met Vardon's son while in residence. It is remarkable to think of Vardon leaving Jersey in 1900 to spend a year touring the United States. Everything about America was different than his homeland, including the rudimentary golf courses he visited. Yet Vardon adjusted to the food, the customs, the travel and the golf, beating nearly everyone he faced and winning the hearts of Americans as he went.

In many ways, Vardon's journey in 1900 paved the way for my own exodus in 1967. Befriended by Arnold Palmer and embraced by the crowds at Augusta National, I began a personal odyssey in America, one that would include my own major victory in the 1970 U.S. Open. When I was inducted into the Golf Hall of Fame in 2002, I was asked where I wanted my marker placed in the walk that surrounds the facility. I chose to be near Harry Vardon, a player I have always admired.

Although many know of Vardon's famous defeat by Francis Ouimet at Brookline during the 1913 U.S. Open, few know the details of his extensive trip thirteen years earlier. This book details the men he played, the courses he visited, and the challenges he faced, and in the process reveals an American golf scene at its genesis. In so doing it also honors one of the greatest sportsmen of all time, a Jersey man who conquered the world.

—Tony Jacklin

Preface

In 1899, Harry Vardon had a Tiger Woods–type year. The twenty-nine-year-old dominated the competitive scene, winning nearly 75 percent of the challenge matches and professional tournaments in which he participated. His five-stroke triumph in the Open Championship was his third in four years and marked the first time any golfer had led wire-to-wire in a 72-hole event. A home-and-away challenge match with Willie Park Jr. ended in a humiliating defeat for Park and a £200 prize for Vardon—a highlight of a year in which he made more money from golf than anyone ever had before. The Englishman was at the top of his game and the pinnacle of the sport.

It was due to this background that the American-based Spalding Company offered Vardon a lucrative endorsement contract and a chance to tour America and display his skills against all the top players of the era the following year. Although Park had come to America five years before, his public displays had been confined to a few courses in the Northeast, while most of his time was taken up with business pursuits. Vardon's tour was to be the first of its kind—a yearlong extravaganza that would bring the best golfer in the world to as many venues as possible—or at least those that had the $250 appearance fee Vardon commanded.

From February to December, with six weeks off in May and June to defend his British Open championship back at St. Andrews, Vardon toured America, playing nearly every top golfer, amateur or professional. He played the three previous U.S. Amateur champions and four of the first five U.S. Open winners. He played transplanted Scots such as Alex Findlay, who had been in the country since the 1880s, and the most recent arrivals, like Robert White in Cincinnati.

As you can see from the photographs, he played in places that were barely recognizable as golf courses. Most had nine holes; many were less than 2,500 yards long. They had clay greens, sand greens, or dirt greens—some had little grass anywhere on the layout. Few were turfed like the British courses he had grown up on, and many of the bump-and-run shots he had relied on were useless given the nature of the ground. After his initial shock, Vardon adapted and still dominated.

You can also see that Vardon was a trendsetter in more ways than one. In the 1890s knickers were not unknown, but they were mostly reserved for children's garb. When Vardon appeared at a tournament in Ireland wearing plus-fours, knee socks, Norfolk jacket, and tie he was ridiculed. Not only did this grouping become his signature outfit, it had become the standard golfing attire of the day within a few years, and it remained so for decades to come.

It's hard for today's player to understand what golf was like for the masses in this era and how advanced Vardon's game was. When Vardon hit the ball 200 yards off the tee he outdistanced nearly every professional he played against. When he hit it 230 yards, that was the longest drive anyone had ever seen. The average amateur of 1900 hit the ball about 150 yards when he caught it well. And getting to a green in regulation on a 250-yard hole was not an easy task, given the small-headed, smooth-faced irons most golfers used.

Once a golfer was on the green, putting on the rough, shaggy surfaces that were little different from the fairway was an adventure. Any putt over fifteen feet that was holed was newsworthy, and making four-footers was far from a given. Vardon was not the best putter among the pros, and it was considered the weak part of his otherwise outstanding game. He clearly dominated his peers with his driving and approach shots; around the greens he was human, and that's where he was beaten on the rare occasions that happened.

Vardon lost at least fifteen times over the course of eighty-some matches. But most of those losses came against the best ball of two professionals, or of the best amateurs of the region. Only twice was he beaten head-to-head, and both times it was by the same man. Bernard Nicholls became something of a celebrity when he got the better of Vardon at Ormond Beach in Florida and later at Brae Burn in Massachusetts. While Vardon took it in stride, Nicholls parlayed his victories into appearances in Great Britain—though he never lived up to the hype in his subsequent matches against British and Scottish pros.

Most stops Vardon made involved a practice match the day prior to the official match—and often the only difference between the two was that Vardon's stipend was paid only on the second day. Some of the practice games were foursomes or best-ball competitions where Vardon teamed with a local amateur versus the host pro and a club champion. Although we need not mimic Vardon's outdated techniques, one thing we can learn from these encounters, and from the main events as well, was the speed of play. Most matches were concluded in well under two hours. Unlike today, when we wait endlessly for a pro to analyze a putt from six directions or check the wind, the ball, and the rotation of the earth before playing an approach shot, the spectators in 1900 had trouble keeping up with the match. And although Vardon brought the golfing spectacle to thousands during his tour, actual crowd sizes were usually in the 250- to 750-person range. In 1900, getting a thousand people to a golf course, even to see the world champion, was a considerable achievement.

One hundred and seven years later, it is amazing how many clubs there are where no one knows that Vardon once graced the property. Some of the finest private courses in America fail to make a single mention of his visit in their club history books. Even up until the final week of writing this book, I was still uncovering matches Vardon played during the year. So the odds are that I have missed one or two, but it's not for lack of trying. I have combed newspapers, magazines, books, journals, and club handbooks to complete the picture. All of the post-tour recaps that detail his travels are different, so piecing together the puzzle was a task in itself.

Though some of the games remain a mystery, for a majority of the matches I have far more information than I've presented. Often I have a stroke-by-stroke account, but if I were to reproduce all the details, the book could be sold as a sleep aid rather than as a chronicle of an amazing pilgrimage. If you'd like to know more about a specific event, please be in touch. I'd be happy to share the details with you.

Meanwhile, sit back and enjoy a snapshot of one year in early American golf. It was a time when you put on a jacket and tie, took a train to your club, grabbed a bag full of wooden sticks, found your regular caddie, and set off for a quick walk chasing a ball made of tree sap over a golf course that was less manicured than today's highway median.

This posed picture of Vardon ran in newspapers
on both sides of the Atlantic in 1899.

CHAPTER 1

Hello, America!

A Relaxing Passage

When Harry Vardon stepped off the saloon passengers' gangplank of the *St. Paul* ocean liner on Saturday, February 3, 1900, and onto the docks of New York harbor he was twenty-nine years old, 5′ 11″ tall, 155 pounds, with an athletic build and excellent balance. He was without an ounce of fat; *Golf Illustrated* described him as "hard as nails in condition, very sinewy and as active as a sprinter in moving about." Augmenting his classic good looks, he sported a mustache, and short brown hair to match his eyes, turning many a young woman's head. "Vardon has the winning ways to charm a Duchess if he cared to try," claimed George Low, one of the foremost golf professionals in America.

The weeklong Atlantic crossing had been pleasantly free of storms, and Vardon had time to relax and contemplate what lay ahead. "The idea of a trip to the United States appealed to me very strongly," wrote Vardon. "I was anxious to see this great country, and apart from the financial benefit which I should derive from the tour, fully expected to enjoy, to me, the novel experience of visiting a strange land."

The reigning "Champion Golfer of the Year" wore a long blue cloth coat lined and trimmed with squirrel's fur, a soft brown Alpine hat, a gray suit, and tan shoes, and he carried a shawl but no luggage. He was met at the American Line pier by Charles Cox, the reigning club champion from the Fairfield County Country Club in Greenwich, Connecticut, who was to serve as Vardon's manager and agent for the yearlong extravaganza. Cox had been to the Open Championship and witnessed Vardon's precision. "I saw Vardon play, and a more perfect machine it is impossible to imagine," said Cox. "Such extraordinary straight driving and straight approaching it is difficult to conceive unless one sees his work."

The two exchanged greetings as Vardon's luggage was assembled, including a long leather case that held thirteen precious golf clubs. In contrast to the massive arsenals toted by many an American tyro, the

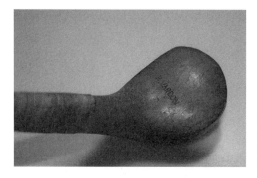

Vardon's personal clubs were unique, featuring small heads made of dogwood and stamped with his name.

The face on Vardon's driver was barely as tall as the height of a golf ball.

three-time British champion used only seven clubs when playing the links. "They are all beauties," he said of his implements, "the pick of nearly four hundred that I have used at different times." The leather box contained two drivers, one brassey, two driving mashies, two cleeks, two putters, a niblick, two lofters, and a "special club of his own make, having a deep face resembling the driving mashie." The *New York Sun* continued, "One of the putters is known as a goose-neck putter, from the shape of the iron above the head. That putter Vardon would not part with for many times its original cost, for he has had it three years, and used it in two of his Open championship victories. He generally uses a cleek for a long putt and the goose-neck for putting on the green. Unlike many foreign players, Vardon does not use a wooden putter." On the customs form Vardon listed the hickory sticks as "the tools of his trade," and officials passed them on free of duty.

Hailing from the tiny town of Grouville on the rural island of Jersey off the English coast, Vardon had toured much of the United Kingdom playing golf. But he had yet to see anything like New York City, a metropolis of three million people. Vardon and Cox were taken to the Broadway Central Hotel, where they would base their operations when playing courses in the area, and the visitor was immediately overwhelmed by reporters. "This was an experience which I am not likely to forget," Vardon wrote in his 1933 autobiography, *My Golfing Life*. "Anyone who has not been interviewed by an American news-paper 'man' will possibly fail to realize how extremely careful it is to be when discussing anything with them." Vardon would become used to seeing statements he had allegedly made on the front pages of the nation's papers, and he realized that even when he held his tongue the reporters were not above putting words in his mouth. On this occasion he had nothing but praise for America and hope for a successful tour—after the buildup in the press, the American public was anxious to hear anything from this golfing god.

"The personal appearance of any hero is always interesting," wrote the *New York Sun*. "It may be stated at once that Vardon car-ries none of the marks of his three championships on the exterior. Many a one-year amateur is far more pompous in his golfing talk and regalia than is Vardon. No one could be more modest than he. His frank, clear-cut face lights up easily with a cheerful smile, and, although his reputation as a talker is not great, he replies readily and to the point to all questions."

Vardon was not so cheerful in private, however, dealing with the heat in his hotel room. "On going to my bedroom on that first evening in New York, I soon became acquainted with the American system of heating their rooms. As I prepared for bed the heat of the room was fast becoming exceedingly oppressive. The steam pipes were hissing away, and no doubt I could, with a little manipulation, very easily could have turned them off. As it was however, I did not care, in my ignorance, to play about with them. Eventually, above the door, I saw a glass partition, which after a little while I was able to open, and so obtain a little relief from a situation which was becom-ing almost unbearable." Vardon survived the first night's sauna but nearly lost his shoes in the process. In the finer British hotels it was custom to leave one's shoes outside the door for overnight clean-ing. "My surprise may be very easily judged when the porter asked me if I wished them thrown away … and added that anything put outside the door of one's room was considered of no further use to the owner, and was thrown away."

Vardon saved his shoes and put them to good use the following day. He was fascinated by the tall buildings of the city and spent Sunday touring the sights. New York was a symphony of sounds, smells, and activity new to the champion, and he soaked it in like millions of tourists since. In the evening it was off to vaudeville, a much different form of entertainment from the music halls of home. Vardon had always been fascinated by the theatre and music, but as with many other things, American big-city nightlife was a world away from the common amusements in rural England. Vardon was captivated.

On Monday the business of the trip began, and he was off to Chicopee, Massachusetts, to visit with his sponsors, the Spalding Company. Spalding had been encouraged to bring Vardon to America by Julian Curtiss, and there is conflicting information regarding their exact arrangements. It is quite possible that a final face-to-face negotiation was convened in Chicopee between Vardon, Cox, Curtiss, and Spalding.

After the meeting Vardon was reunited with Alex Findlay, a Spalding professional who had represented Wright & Ditson Sporting Goods before that company had been absorbed by Spalding. Findlay had met Vardon in England the previous fall and was one of the main proponents of a tour in America. Vardon had delivered the only defeat of Findlay's tour, and the two would face off more than any other opponents over the next year. "Let me in a few words give you an idea of what Harry is like," Findlay said to the press in Chicopee. "In the first place he differs from me very much, as he is quite nice looking, and is greatly admired by the ladies. I drive a fairly good ball; he drives a better. I don't mean quality, I mean distance. Vardon is exceptionally quiet and unassuming, free from the wickedness and vices that often beset young golf professionals. He smokes a briar pipe all the while during a friendly match. He is passionately fond of golf and association football." The sport known as football, that we later termed soccer, had barely gained a foothold in America; Vardon was a member of a local team in his homeland and played regular league games during the winter months.

Vardon and Findlay toured the manufacturing facility in Massachusetts, inspecting the Vardon Flyer ball and the Vardon line of clubs he was in America to promote. Spalding traced its business roots to 1876 when Albert Goodwill Spalding opened a small sporting goods store in Chicago. The company expanded to the East Coast in 1885, selling gear for baseball, football, bicycling, and tennis.

In the early 1890s, director Julian Curtiss imported golf clubs from Scotland, and subsequently a line of golf products was added to the company's offerings. When Spalding bought a bicycle manufacturing

Financial Arrangements

What financial gain Harry Vardon realized from his relationship with Spalding and his trip to America in general was the subject of great interest and speculation in both the American and British press. With direct quotes from Spalding, his manager, and his biographer in conflict with one another, it is hard to know the truth of the matter. Vardon never addressed the issue through interviews at the time, and he was probably ill at ease in discussing it both privately and publicly.

His income as a teenage gardener was about £16 a year. His professional golf winnings during 1899 reached £500. To leave his wife comfortable at home, travel to America and back twice during the course of ten months, arrange for all his transport, food and accommodations in the United States, and realize a profit for his labors required a considerable sum of money.

From accounts in many club history books it is clear that each club needed to pony up at least $250 to bring Vardon to its door. This guaranteed club members a thirty-six-hole match against the players of their choice. The amateur opponents expected no monetary gain for their efforts, but some pros wondered what would be their reward should they beat the champion. Vardon refused any match where he received under $200, or when the outcome determined his paycheck.

As to Vardon's financial arrangement with Spalding, here there are wide discrepancies. "Rumor has it that Spalding paid him the sum of £1,000, plus traveling expenses, and if this is true, it was a vast sum of money for that period," wrote Audrey Howell in her 1988 book about her father-in-law, *Harry Vardon: The Revealing Story of a Champion Golfer.*

In 1900, the British weekly *Golf Illustrated* cited multiple sources in England that claimed an even larger honorarium, around £800 a year for four years. "He is the best golfer that the world has produced. Still, eight hundred a year, which, after all, is only going to mean part of the year, if we understand aright an arrangement that it certainly is none of our business to understand, sounds good; there are critics who write as if it were monstrously excessive."

Josiah Newman, editor of *Golf* magazine in the United States, spent considerable time with Vardon while he was based in New York, and he disputed claims of large sums of money being paid for Vardon's services. "I don't know where you obtained your information about Vardon getting £800 a year from Spalding for four years, but I can say that it is entirely incorrect. Vardon has no contract with Spalding to get anything. That I know absolutely and am authorized so to state both by Vardon and Spalding."

The *New York Times* had another take on the arrangement in an April 29, 1900, article titled "Vardon's Profitable Golf," published just before he returned to England after the first part of his tour. "Three months' work, or rather three months' sport, for $6,750 is the conservative estimate that may be placed to the financial credit of Harry Vardon. How much of this American coin will the Englishman carry back to his home when he finishes his career here? This question has occasioned many interesting speculations. From the best available information, Vardon receives $6,000 as his annual stipend for golf exhibitions and the use of his name."

Charles Cox, who acted as Vardon's manager throughout the year for Spalding, felt that discussion of the financial matters by the press was "mere supposition." In the *Times* he stated, "Only one person knows what the clubs have paid Vardon and that is myself, and the money goes into a 'special fund.' We have no contract of any description with Vardon."

While some "authorities" claim Vardon received pay for each match and paid his own expenses, and others "in the know" claimed a lump sum outlay, Vardon offered this in his book *My Golfing Life*, written thirty-three years later. "Towards the end of the year [1899] A. G. Spaldings made me an offer for an extended tour in the United States. They suggested they would give me a fixed sum for every exhibition match in which I took part, and of course pay all my expenses. This included a first-class return passage to America, all hotel accommodation, and, in fact, all expenses from the moment of leaving England until my return. Although I made up my mind to accept the offer which had been made to me, I came to the conclusion that instead of receiving so much for every match which I took part in, I would rather receive a lump sum to cover all my engagements. Spaldings were quite willing to agree to this arrangement."

Vardon felt he would have made more on a match-by-match basis, but he wanted the security of a lump sum, in part so he could set up his wife with a comfortable living situation before he left and not have to worry during his travels. Whatever the ultimate reward for Vardon he called it "the most interesting experience of my career." And it's a good bet that during 1900 the humble man from Jersey made more money from golf than any other person on the planet.

plant in Chicopee, the company had the capacity to make its own clubs in America, and starting in 1897 offered the hand-forged "The Spalding" brand. By 1900, Spalding was turning out thousands of clubs and balls for the burgeoning U.S. market. Having been a

Vardon Clubs and the Vardon Flyer

When Spalding entered into an agreement with Vardon to tour the United States, the company also obtained the rights to produce both a Vardon line of golf clubs and a ball that they felt confident they could market to the growing legion of American players. Although Vardon produced results far beyond those of any other golfers with both products, he would have been greatly disappointed if his financial future had revolved around royalties from sales. Both ball and clubs were outdated shortly after their introduction and never produced the economic windfall Spalding hoped for.

The Vardon Flyer was the most scientifically advanced gutta-percha ball of all those in use for nearly half a century. But even before it was produced, the rubber-core Haskell ball had been developed, and that "Bounding Billy" would completely replace the solid gutta design. In its 1900 catalogue, Spalding claimed, "Vardon's own ball, manufactured in England for him from 'Special Gutta' is without doubt the longest flying ball in the market

"The Vardon Flyer"

Vardon's own ball, manufactured in England for him from "Special Gutta," is without doubt the longest flying ball in the market to-day. It is a Bramble-marked ball. Vardon claims for this marking a longer and truer flight than can be obtained from the smooth markings, and that this opinion is not theoretical, but practical, is proved by the fact that he out-drives every man he meets, has broken or tied the record on every course he has played, and has never touched 80 in twenty-six consecutive 36-hole matches. The man, we know, is all right, and the above facts make us think that the ball is second only to the man.

"The Vardon Flyer" is never sent out until thoroughly seasoned, and for uniformity of weight and perfection of flight is not equalled by any ball on the market. Per Dozen, $4.00.

A. G. SPALDING & BROS.
New York   Chicago   Denver

It was difficult to debate Spalding's claim that Vardon hit the Flyer farther than anyone else; the only caveat was that he could also accomplish that feat with any other ball as well.

VARDON CLUBS

A MAN to make a name in the world must have a marked individuality: the mechanic who suddenly becomes an expert usually attains that position by the use or invention of some Special Tool.

Vardon Clubs have an individuality which no other clubs possess, and betray in their make and peculiarities the clever brain which conceived them and the common-sense principles which are the secrets of his marvellous success as a golfer.

Every club is as perfect as the most critical workmanship can make it, and any one who has been fortunate enough to see him play must realize that his wonderful accuracy would be impossible unless the clubs were mechanically as perfect as we claim.

A. G. SPALDING & BROS.
New York   Chicago   Denver

The Vardon clubs were small-headed and difficult for the average amateur to hit—a fact that was discovered after they were purchased.

today. It is a bramble-marked ball. Vardon claims for this marking a longer and truer flight than can be obtained from the smooth markings." Another ad stated that "on the average, he out drove every man he met," a claim that could not be disputed by anyone who saw him play.

The balls sold for $4.00 a dozen, about half what the new rubber-cores went for in their first few years, and they sold well—for a short time. Vardon won the 1900 U.S. Open with the ball, but by a year later nearly every U.S. pro had converted to the Haskell ball, and in another year's time Spalding was selling more rubber-cores than gutties. Though the Vardon Flyer continued to be used for practice, Spalding had discontinued manufacturing the spheroid by 1905.

Vardon's clubs were unique, being short, small-headed, and mostly smooth-faced. Walter Travis claimed the heads were made of dogwood, but when Spalding copied them they used hickory. Of his clubs, Spalding wrote: "He is in love with them and never changes the models of either his drivers or his irons from one year's end to another. We have taken his bag of playing clubs and duplicated every one exactly. The wood is selected and must be perfectly seasoned. The grain just right and the hang and the balance perfect or they cannot leave our factory. He will personally inspect every one, and will not permit that 'H. Vardon' shall be stamped on a single club until he is satisfied that in every respect it is worthy of his name."

The Vardon set included eleven clubs—and of the irons all but two, a lofter and a niblick, were smooth faced. "I use the lofter when I have to, and then I think the roughened face helps to hold the ball," Vardon told *Golf Illustrated.* "That's why, too, that I have a corrugated face on the niblick."

VARDON FLYER

The Vardon Flyer

The Vardon Flyer enjoyed one year of commercial success before it was replaced with the longer rubber-core ball.

Today, a Vardon Flyer with original paint may command a price of $1,500 among serious golf ball collectors.

The woods featured a leather insert to soften the feel and sound as they struck the gutty ball—and to keep the head from cracking after repeated blows to the rock-hard gutty.

Many amateurs may have purchased the small-headed Vardon clubs after seeing him play, though few could wield them like the champion. Smooth faces were supplanted by grooves early in the twentieth century; leather replaced by a multitude of materials as technology marched forward.

clubmaker for many years, Vardon was especially interested in the mass-production techniques being employed by the firm and the products that bore his name.

Returning to New York, Vardon was taken to Garden City Golf Club by Josiah Newman, editor of *Golf* magazine. Garden City had one of the most sophisticated layouts in the country at that time and had just been named as the site of the 1900 U.S. Amateur tournament. It was there that Vardon met Walter J. Travis, and the *New York Sun* reported that they "played over a part of the course." Vardon was quoted as saying, "Why, this is grand: this is like Sandwich. Really, although I have heard a great deal of your courses, I did not think you had anything quite as fine as this. It's well suited for any championship tournament."

In 1900, Garden City Golf Club was one of the most sophisticated links in the country.

Opening Encounter: February 12, 1900

If Vardon thought that every course in America was of the quality of Garden City, his beliefs were shattered the next day when he arrived at the site of his first official match. The location of the fledgling Laurence Harbor Golf Club was stunning: high on a bluff near Perth Amboy, New Jersey, overlooking the tip of Staten Island and Raritan Bay. But, according to the *New York Times,* "the artistic delights of the place were badly dimmed yesterday by a raw Scotch mist." Considering that it was early February in the Northeast, the gloomy weather should not have been a surprise. But the appearance of the one-year-old, nine-hole course, designed by Willie Dunn Jr. may have been. "The condition of the links was also lamentable," continued the *Times.* "The damp weather and the constant use to which they had been put the previous two days had made them as soggy as a suburban town in the opening of spring. One green of the nine was dry." In *My Golfing Life,* Vardon recalled, "I remember that the clay greens were in such a state that temporary ones had to be made."

The *Times* continued: "Vardon's famous approach pitches onto the green failed absolutely of their effect, only once in a while getting a very little roll. It was necessary to make a special rule—that when the ball fell into a particularly bad spot, so as to be almost buried in the mud, it could be lifted without penalty."

This was the first of many incidents where special rules were made—something that disturbed Vardon, eventually leading him to speak out about American standards in regards to the rules of the game. The *Chicago Tribune* reported another unfathomable incident during the match: "Playing the fourth hole coming home Vardon topped his drive and landed in a gully. The hole is 270 yards long, and this was the only bad drive Vardon made during the day. His opponent told him to lift the ball out and tee it up. Vardon looked at President Freeland in astonishment, saying, 'I have a niblick.' He then played his niblick shot from what looked like an impossible tee [sic], and, to the astonishment of all who were following the match, the ball landed upon the green and halved the hole in four. It was a grand display of skill and thoroughly appreciated."

In addition to the disappointing course and weather, Vardon's opponents were not what would be expected for the opening of such a grand tour, probably owing to the fact that all the top golfers of the region were already down in Florida where it was far more sensible to play in February. Amateurs M. M. Singer of Monmouth Golf Club

Laurence Harbor Golf Club was barely a year old when Vardon played the opening match of his tour, and course conditions were far from ideal.

and John M. Ward played in the morning, with N. C. Villepique taking Ward's place in the afternoon. None of the men was from the elite ranks of American players, although over the rest of the year Vardon would play nearly every top professional and amateur in American golf. One of the country's finest players, however, did watch that first match, perhaps not wanting to be embarrassed by playing against Vardon in the opening contest. "Walter J. Travis was there," wrote the *Times*. "That was the limit of star amateurs. Among the others were perhaps 200 golfers who are known to their friends as players of hopeful ambition."

The first tee at Laurence Harbor adjoined the clubhouse piazza, and precisely at ten thirty in the morning Vardon separated from the throng and teed his ball. With little fanfare, and before some of the assembled even realized it, Vardon made the first official swing of his groundbreaking tour. "Vardon had the honor, and drove well, hitting the ball before most of the spectators believed he was ready," reported the *Times*. "In that respect Vardon can teach a valuable lesson to many amateurs who might resent the assertion that their style is not all it might be. Vardon steps up to the ball with ease and

The Laurence Harbor clubhouse overlooked New York harbor.

Features at Laurence Harbor Golf Club were difficult to locate in the Willie Dunn Jr. design.

confidence, plants his feet solidly, takes his club firmly in his overlapping grip, and—swish—the ball is picked up as clean as it could be done with the fingers, and the little white sphere is seen away in the distance flying with the accuracy of a carrier pigeon to its spot."

Though Vardon's technique was a spectacle to behold, the conduct of the match was not. Findlay Douglas, a member of the Laurence Harbor club and Vardon's scheduled nemesis in the contest, was a conspicuous absence; the men who stood in for him were a far cry from his golfing equal and understandably nervous. By the fourth hole Vardon was 3 up, a pattern that would continue, with the morning eighteen ending with the visiting champion up by 8. The best ball of the challengers captured only four of the twenty-seven holes played, the match ending on the eighth green in the afternoon with Vardon 11 up with ten to play. Due to the weather the players did not finish out the match. Vardon took the ninth hole and the day was done.

Less than a year later, the *Times* carried this obituary: "The Laurence Harbor Golf Club, which created a temporary stir in the local golfing world a year or two ago, has sunk into oblivion, and its name has been struck from the metropolitan membership list,

The Vardon Grip

Virtually everyone who is taught golf learns the Vardon grip—a method of holding the golf club that has existed for more than a century. When one thinks of all the techniques that have changed since Vardon's day it is amazing that this concept has persisted.

Vardon did not invent the grip, nor did he ever claim to have. Most historians agree that John Laidlay, a Scottish amateur from the 1870s, was the first to employ it. "Personally, I have not the least doubt that I was the first person to use the grip," Laidlay stated. But James Braid wisely noted that "whoever invented the grip, Vardon was the man who made it popular."

Harry Vardon did not invent the overlapping grip, but the technique has carried his name for more than a century.

Folklore suggests that Vardon utilized the method because he didn't like the knots in the homemade clubs he devised as a kid, or that his hands were so large he couldn't fit them on the handle. Neither is true. "I adopted it only after a careful trial of all the other grips of which I had ever heard, and in my opinion it has contributed materially to the attainment of such skill as I possess," Vardon said. "I believe in it very firmly and advise every golfer to try to accustom himself to it. My contention is that the overlapping grip is sounder in theory and easier in practice, tends to make a better stroke and to secure a straighter ball, and that players who adopt it from the beginning will stand a much better chance of driving well at an early stage than if they went in for the old-fashioned two-V."

The overlapping grip was hardly known when Vardon toured America in 1900; the "baseball grip," with the shaft across the

In addition to using shorter clubs, Vardon choked up on each of them as much as three inches.

palms of both hands and both thumbs wrapping around, was far more common. The grip was just another source of excitement to the fans who looked for any keys that unlocked the secrets of Vardon's talent.

as the merry sound of golf balls is heard no more over its links. The history of this club offers interesting lessons regarding spasmodic efforts to boom a certain locality while there is plenty of real estate to be disposed of."

As much as Vardon loved the excitement of New York City, he was more than happy to pack his bags after the Laurence Harbor debacle and head for warmer climates. In the cold February rain of coastal New Jersey it was hard to imagine the warm delight of southern Florida that awaited him, especially for someone accustomed to the misty moors of the British Isles.

CHAPTER 2

Jersey to New Jersey

Rural Upbringing

How did Harry Vardon arrive at his first match in New Jersey in 1900 as the greatest golfer in the world? It was a unique combination of natural athletic ability, persistence and drive, a pleasant personality, good upbringing, the fortune of an agreeable birthplace, and some dumb luck involving being in the right place at the right time.

Born Henry William Vardon on May 9, 1870, he was always known as Harry. He was the fourth son of Philip and Eliza Vardon; they sired six sons and two daughters in all. His parents were both born and raised on the British island of Jersey, and there they remained to raise their family. His father was first employed in the shipbuilding industry and then worked as a gardener for most of his adult life. Little is known of his mother, for Vardon never mentioned her in interviews or writing, but she certainly had her hands full at home with eight children.

Jersey, the southernmost of the Channel Islands, sits just a few nautical miles from the Normandy coast of France. Lapped by the warm waters of the Portugal current of the Gulf Stream, the island is the warmest spot in England, known for summer temperature records and mild, snowless winters. Although it lies at 50 degrees latitude, the region is temperate, giving birth to an agrarian economy that has supplemented fishing, shipping, and boat building. Blessed with a rich soil atop a limestone substructure, Jersey has long been known for Jersey Royal New Potatoes, tomatoes, cauliflower, flowers, and dairy products from the milk of the namesake Jersey cows.

Harry grew up in a tiny cottage, just 500 yards from the sea, that was surrounded by common land. His mother was of French heritage, his father of English, and both languages were spoken at home, the French being a local Jersey dialect. The tiny town of Grouville was the nearest village, set on the Gorey Bay and within sight of Mont Orgueil Castle.

Philip Vardon was taciturn and strict with his children, working endlessly to feed the family and make ends meet. Harry felt that his

Royal Jersey Golf Club was built on classic links land. The layout bordered the house in which Vardon grew up.

father favored younger brother Tom, who would also go on to become a golf professional—though not with the competitive success Harry enjoyed. Even after Harry had won his third Open Championship his father said, "Harry may win the prizes, but it's Tom who plays the golf."

The family scraped together two pence a week to send Harry to the local school, and he received enough education to be literate—but sitting in an indoor classroom was not part of his nature. Neither was book learning. "It was perhaps only right that I was considered the dunce of the school," Vardon wrote. His punishment for incomplete homework assignments was to clean out the school's rabbit hutches, a task he secretly enjoyed as it removed him from the indoor environment and put him in the outdoors he cherished. He left school for good at age twelve.

Harry excelled at sports in his youth, playing cricket and football with gusto and setting track records as well. His forte was the 150-yard sprint, and he won several prizes on the school's sports days. But the game for which he would be known caught his attention by chance in 1877.

"Golf first came into my life when I was six or seven years old," Vardon wrote in his 1904 autobiography, *My Golfing Life.* "One Sunday

Vardon always enjoyed club football and continued to play in the winter months for years. Here, he is third from the right in the front row.

morning, to the astonishment and indignation of the inhabitants, two strangers appeared at Grouville carrying red flags, with which they marked out a rough course, and proceeded to play a strange and, it seemed, absurd game. There was much shaking of heads and muttering over this desecration of the Sabbath, and the strangers were lucky to get away without being molested. They returned a few days later with other strangers and before long golf was in full swing at Grouville." When the residents learned that their common land would not be harmed and that the players who frequented the links needed caddies, food, and playable surfaces—all which resulted in employment for the locals—the game was accepted.

Athletic by nature, Harry investigated the new sport that had been installed on the natural links land overlooking the sea in his home town. "I was much interested in this new game, and soon made my first attempts at it with a stick and a stone," he wrote. As was common among youths in this era, Vardon made his own primitive clubs from the native trees. He found straight limbs from thorn trees for shafts, with blocks of wood from apple and oak as clubheads. A red hot poker provided a boring for the shaft to connect to the head, and sheepskin formed the grip. When the heads began to crack Vardon covered them in tin and called them "brassies." The clubs would suffice until castoffs from members at the new course were available.

"Then I became a caddie, and off and on I carried until I left Jersey," he later recalled. Vardon made about a sixpence (approximately twelve cents) per round—not bad for a ten-year-old in the early 1880s. A year after the first nine holes were staked, the Jersey Golf Club was given royal status by Queen Victoria, and when the second nine was added the golf course was literally in Vardon's backyard. The twelfth fairway of Royal Jersey bordered his family's property.

With his access to the course on off days Harry's skill developed at a rapid pace. But when he finished his schooling he followed the employment path set by his father and became a gardener for the Spofforth family in town, playing golf as time allowed. At his employer's suggestion Harry joined the Workingman's Club at Grouville and was soon playing at scratch or better, establishing himself as the best player in the club. But Harry stuck with gardening through his teenage years, despite the fact his brother had left home at age sixteen to accept a position as a golf professional at St. Anne's-on-the-Sea. "Having seen me play during his visits home, he advised me to apply for the post of professional to Lord Ripon's private golf course, which he happened to know was vacant. I did so, was engaged, and left Jersey for the first time at the age of twenty."

Part of Tom's convincing argument to leave Jersey came in the form of a letter he sent Harry that described his play in an open tournament for professionals at Musselburgh, Scotland. Tom had finished second and won £12, a staggering sum for the boys from Jersey.

But Philip discouraged his son from leaving. After all, Tom was the outgoing one, Harry quiet and reserved—leading his father to believe Harry lacked the "sufficient keenness" to compete at the highest levels. Harry recognized a chance to get away from his domineering father, as well as to make money with his talent, and he packed his bags. In less than a decade Harry Vardon would be widely acknowledged as the best golfer in the world.

Decade of Accomplishment

From the beginning of 1890 until the end of 1899, Vardon made his way steadily up the ladder of professional golf. His brother had arranged his employment at Lord Ripon's primarily to get Harry out of the family house in Jersey, but it was not the right fit for Vardon.

The lord didn't even play golf himself, and the course was a luxury for his visitors and friends. Harry found himself playing far more cricket than golf, as that was what interested the other employees on the estate, and Harry was always up for a competitive game, no matter what the sport. But being on his own for the first time, and lacking the sense of self-discipline he would later develop, Vardon failed to advance his golf game. When he realized his economic well-being was tied to his skills, Vardon knew it was time to move to a more golf-oriented environment.

After a year at the Ripon estate, he landed a job at the Bury Golf Club, a nine-hole layout cut from a farmer's field. Between these jobs, Vardon returned to Jersey, where he met Jessie Bryant. Their relationship advanced rather quickly: shortly after he arrived at his new position at Bury, Vardon received a letter from Jessie announcing her pregnancy.

A hasty wedding took place on November 15, 1891, but, with impending child, Jessie had no interest in accompanying Harry to Bury. She remained with her family as Harry headed off to a hectic position where he was expected to maintain the golf course, repair and make golf clubs, give lessons to the members, and work on his own game. Quite a load for a young man away from home, especially coming off his low-key arrangement at Ripon, and with a wife expecting a child far away. His personal life took the first of many downward steps when his son, Clarence Henry Vardon, died at six weeks old, throwing his young wife into a depression she would fight for decades.

Jessie not only refused to accompany Harry back to Bury; she seldom left her room over the following year. Harry had no choice but to throw himself back into his work, practicing his game with diligence in the three-and-a-half years he remained at Bury. Vardon never took a lesson in his life, developing his talent at an early age through practice. His elegant upright swing ended in a violent descending blow that allowed Vardon to hit the ball high and soft with bite, in sharp contrast to the ground game that was prevalent in his day. The widely practiced St. Andrews' school of technique involved sweeping the ball from the top of the grass plant, producing a low running shot.

Vardon joined his brother Tom at the 1893 Open Championship at Prestwick, giving him his first chance to compare his game to those of the golfing greats of the late nineteenth century. He had played one professional tournament previously—that at Kilmacomb near Paisley,

The Englishman perfected his game with endless practice—and then had little use for it during his best years.

Scotland. "I think it was pretty bold of me, a Southerner, to go and tackle the Scotsmen in their own country at the first attempt. Fernie was first, Herd second, and I was quite satisfied to be for third place. It was the first time I had seen the 'crack' professional players, and I need hardly say I was greatly impressed by their skill," Vardon wrote. At Prestwick, Harry finished twenty-two strokes off the winning score of Laurie Auchterlonie, but one in front of his brother, a pattern that would continue throughout their professional lives.

Vardon continued to improve his game, and early in 1896 he took his third professional post at a five-year-old, eighteen-hole course in Ganton, a course designed by H. S. Colt and Alister Mackenzie. He rented a small cottage near the course and finally convinced his wife to join him; Jessie once again became pregnant around the first of the year. But by spring she had miscarried, and the personal lives of the Vardons were far from what they had envisioned. Jessie again fell into a depression, and without her family at hand there was little to console her.

In this era, besides the Open Championship, challenge matches were the most important measure of a player's talents. With the 1896 championship looming, J. H. Taylor came to Ganton to play Vardon and, in Taylor's words, "he made mincemeat of me." Taylor's warning that Vardon was the man to reckon with at the Open proved accurate just a few weeks later.

On September 1, 1896, Harry Vardon won his first Open Championship, beating J. H. Taylor in a play-off at Muirfield. Tom finished tenth, nine strokes behind Harry, and then grabbed his bag and caddied for him in the play-off. Harry won £30 for his triumph—at a time when £1 was a good weekly wage. "No golf could have borne the impress of more cool self-confidence than the game Vardon showed in playing off for the great prize," wrote Horace Hutchinson. "Taylor

Tom Vardon

Thomas Alfred Vardon was born two years after his more famous brother. Tom turned pro earlier and took several posts in England including St. Anne's on the Sea from 1888 to 1890, Ilkley from 1890 to 1893, and Royal St. George's from 1893 to 1900.

Tom was outgoing and jovial, possessing a wealth of golfing talent with an equal dose of social skills. He encouraged Harry to ply his talents as a professional golfer and to leave bucolic Jersey where they had grown up. Some reports credit Tom not only with encouraging Harry to apply for his first pro position at Lord Ripon's estate, but also with working behind the scenes to make sure he was hired.

Harry's younger brother, Tom, turned professional at age sixteen, and his earnings from competition convinced Harry it was the path he too should follow.

Tom entered his first Open Championship in 1891, tying for ninth at St. Andrews. The winnings he amassed as a teenager convinced Harry to give up his career as a gardener in Jersey and become a professional golfer. "I knew in my own heart I was quite as good as my brother," wrote Harry, "and that if he could win such sums of money as this, there could be no reason why I should not be able to do the same."

The two traveled together in the early years, and Tom brought Harry to his first Open at Prestwick in 1893. Ten years later, Tom enjoyed his best finish in the Open by placing second at Prestwick, six strokes behind his brother, who won the championship for the fourth time. Tom came to America for a visit in 1909, returning as the golf professional at Onwentsia near Chicago in 1911 and then enjoying a twenty-two-year tenure at White Bear Yacht Club in Minnesota. He competed in the U.S. Open on multiple occasions; his best finish was a tie for ninth in 1916 at Minikahda Country Club in Minneapolis.

played well, considering he had so much to lose and comparatively so little to win in the way of reputation. But Vardon played better; especially he putted better. The manner in which he won the match, the perfect coolness, the perfect absence of swagger, yet the perfect

Vardon was employed at the Ganton Golf Club in 1900. He was
granted a leave of absence to tour the United States.

possession of confidence, these are very typical of the player and
of his style."

"That, I think, was the most exciting competition I have ever
taken part in," Vardon wrote a decade later. It was the first of six such
victories overall, three of which he would amass before he came to
America in 1900.

A new generation of players was emerging. Although the term
would not be used for a few years yet, the "Great Triumvirate" was
laying the groundwork for their amazing dominance of golf in the
United Kingdom. Between 1894 and 1914, Harry Vardon, J. H. Taylor,
and James Braid won all but five of the twenty-one Opens played. Had
the championship not been suspended in 1915 for five years due to
World War I they undoubtedly would have won several more.

Vardon was also setting a standard in another way: he influenced
how golf professionals dressed when demonstrating their skills.
Accustomed to hand-me-down clothes in his youth, Vardon was
thrifty as a young professional. But as his income increased he found
a liking for fine-quality clothing and had his suits made to order. In
1897, when he appeared at a tournament at Royal Portrush in a new

costume that distinguished him from the other competitors, it caused quite a commotion. "The professionals dressed to play in ordinary clothes, long trousers and an old coat," wrote Portrush member Dr. Taggart. "All except Harry Vardon who had the cheek to play in knickerbockers and a Norfolk jacket. Such a thing was then unheard-of among professionals and it was a piece of what they looked on as snobbery."

Though the professionals may have been offended by Vardon's style of dress, he found it eminently practical. Knickerbockers, or plus fours (so named because the pants extended four inches beyond the knee), were common attire for teenage boys. But Vardon complained that long pants dragged in the mud and became rumpled, even suggesting that his Scottish competitors might consider kilts—their traditional formal attire— as another suitable alternative to full-length pants. Few took the bait.

But Vardon persisted. The outfit he debuted at Portrush became his signature, and he wore it with style for the rest of his career. The Irish

Before 1897, when Vardon appeared at a tournament at Royal Portrush wearing knickers and a Norfolk jacket, the attire was reserved mostly for children. The style became popular with golfers and remained the preferred outfit for decades to come.

newspapers lambasted him, and others followed, but a year later his outfits were available throughout the United Kingdom and worn by many Vardon followers. And after he won the Portrush tournament by eleven strokes, there was little criticism to be heard.

Every appointment of the outfit had a purpose. His white shirt featured a starched one-inch collar; any higher and he believed it restricted his neck and rubbed when he followed through with his swing. He believed in braces (the British term for suspenders) rather than a belt, claiming they reminded him to keep his shoulders upright and square. But he demanded the braces be well used and broken in, rather than new and rigid. "I would no more think of going out

Willie Park Jr.

Although he was only six years older than Harry Vardon, Willie Park Jr. represented the old guard in British Isles golf, while Vardon heralded the new. Park had dominated the years before Vardon's ascendancy, winning the Open Championship in 1887 and 1889 as well as numerous challenge matches before turning his attention to family business interests. Park was a club- and ball-maker, professional instructor, golf course architect (with offices on two continents), book author, and one-time real estate developer.

Willie Park Jr. put aside competitive golf to concentrate on the family business of clubmaking and course design.

From a young age, Park tinkered with the design of golf clubs, looking for ways to improve both his game and others'. In 1892, Park patented the first of many clubs he would invent. Park's Patent Putter was deemed a "wry-necked abortion" in some circles, but the putter worked, and it bears an uncanny resemblance to offset putters still being produced today.

Vardon's 1899 challenge match against Willie Park Jr. attracted the largest crowd ever to witness a golf game, and resulted in a humiliating defeat for Park.

He also wrote with authority. Published in April 1896, *The Game of Golf* was the first book written by a playing golf professional and was hailed by *Golfing* magazine as "a triumph of simple language." It offered sound advice on playing the game, choosing the right club, evaluating your opponent, the proper display of etiquette, determining handicaps, employment of caddies, and the laying out of courses, and it included a "Glossary of Technical Terms."

Park came to America in 1895 as a guest of the members at St. Andrew's in Yonkers, New York, made another visit in 1896 to set up a clubmaking business in New York City, and then returned to Great Britain for twenty years. Although Park displayed golfing skills no one could emulate in his two early visits, few Americans had a chance to follow him in competition as they did with Vardon because he confined his play to a sparse schedule in the Northeast. When Park arrived again in 1916 he set about designing golf courses throughout North America, including highly regarded layouts for Mt. Bruno Country Club outside of Montreal, Woodway in Connecticut, and Olympia Fields near Chicago.

to play for a championship in a new pair of braces than of trying to do the four rounds on my head," Vardon claimed.

He never wore a golf glove, even after they became common in the 1920s. His large fleshy hands allowed solid contact with the club, and he saw no need for a layer between skin and leather. He kept a half dozen pairs of golf shoes of different styles in his closet, but all with the same nail pattern hammered into the sole. His knee-length socks were wool, and his jacket allowed freedom of movement but hung stylishly.

As with any change in the fashion norm, there were criticisms of his appearance—mainly from the men he beat so handily. Vardon took them in stride and let his play speak for him. Coupled with his good looks, Vardon's natty outfits did attract the female contingent, something he likely enjoyed given the depressing nature of his marriage.

For all his success in 1896 through 1898, it was his exploits of 1899 that cemented his status as the greatest golfer in the world. In the 1898 Open Championship at Prestwick, Willie Park Jr. arrived at the final green needing only a two-putt to tie Vardon and force a play-off. In uncharacteristic fashion Park three-putted, and Vardon had his second Claret Jug.

Park did not take the defeat well and issued a challenge to Vardon for a 72-hole match: 36 holes in Scotland and 36 in England. The two men represented far more than just their different homelands. Born in Musselburgh, Park was an intelligent business owner who designed and manufactured golf clubs, planned courses, and promoted himself and his company throughout Europe. He employed the standard St. Andrews swing that kept the ball low and moved it right to left, achieving his distance with the hooking spin that propelled the ball rapidly along the ground.

The open putting stance of a young Harry Vardon.

Vardon was the new Englishman with an upright swing and an aerial approach, lofting the ball high and imparting backspin that often stopped approach shots dead in their tracks. He dressed well, spoke modestly, and was content to limit his activities to competitions and his role as club professional. At a time when the winner of the Open Championship claimed £40 for his triumph, the challenge match was for £200 ... winner take all.

Sources claim that up to 10,000 spectators came to the 36-hole contest at North Berwick, Scotland. With such a throng following just two competitors, flags were raised at the conclusion of each hole to inform the public who had won. At day's end Vardon was 2 up, giving him a distinct advantage when the match moved to Ganton.

"At Ganton, especially from the back tees, it was necessary to hit the ball for carry," wrote Vardon. "This was my natural method. Park, however, played as was the custom with all the old type of Scottish golfers, a low ball with a draw. The player who adopted this method of driving, where long carries were necessary, was at a distinct disadvantage. The first three holes at Ganton demanded long carries from the back tees and, for this reason, unless Park did not try to draw his drives, I felt I should win all of these three holes." That is exactly what happened, with Park finding the hazard each time and Vardon standing 5 up in the match on the fourth tee. He would cruise to a devastating 11-and-10 defeat of Park.

Vardon won the Open by five strokes over Jack White that year and dominated the tournament circuit all summer and fall, winning fifteen tournaments and challenge matches and amassing a veritable fortune in winnings. For many years afterward, he considered his win over Park as one of the most memorable in his career, for it validated his style of play, signaled a change in the world golfing order, and delighted the followers of British golf. It was with this wind in his sails that Harry Vardon began his voyage to America.

Vardon and the Press

Vardon's tour of America was not only the biggest sports story in 1900, it was one of the most widely covered news events of the year. The media frenzy started even before he arrived, as Spalding placed advertisements in many American newspapers proclaiming 1899 as "The Vardon Year" and Harry as "the greatest golfer that ever lived." The proclamation was intended to sell golf clubs with drivers and brassies fetching $2.50, irons $2.00.

Once he made land, many of his matches were followed by reporters from the *New York Times, Boston Globe, Washington Post, Chicago Tribune*, and a wealth of other major and local newspapers, in addition to *Golf* magazine, Britain's *Golf Illustrated*, and other national magazines of the day. Yet there was still a great deal of misinformation circulating. Just three weeks before his arrival, the venerable *New York Times* still had his name wrong, headlining an article "Awaiting Varden's Arrival."

Vardon was very cautious about what he said to the press because his words often were distorted, altered, or sensationalized. He learned this very early in

The year 1899 was known as

The
Vardon Year

The statement that "he is the greatest golfer that ever lived" is unchallenged on either side of the water. He himself states that some part of his success is due to the peculiar clubs he uses. He is in love with them and never changes the models of either his drivers or his irons from one year's end to another. We have taken his bag of playing clubs and duplicated everyone exactly. The wood is selected and must be perfectly seasoned. The grain just right and the hang and the balance perfect or they cannot leave our factory. He will personally inspect every one and will not permit that "H. VARDON" shall be stamped on a single club until he is satisfied that in every respect it is worthy of his name. The finish of these clubs will be the best which it is possible to put on, with due regard to the fact that they are intended for practical use, not ornament.

PRICES—Drivers and Brassies, $2.50; Irons, $2.00
EVERY CLUB CARRIES OUR FULLEST GUARANTEE

A. G. SPALDING & BROS.
NEW YORK   CHICAGO   DENVER

Vardon dominated golf in 1899 and parlayed that into endorsement contracts and appearance fees that surpassed the income of any other sporting star.

his tour and wrote, "Certainly the American reporters made me gasp at first with their 'interviews,' which usually consisted of repeating things I had not said, and had never dreamed of saying, and very personal and most incorrect details about myself, my family, and my doings in general. However, I got used to them, and had many a laugh over the mistakes they made in describing matches."

In light of Vardon's observations one must be careful in reading too much into the quotes attributed to the champion. Vardon offered these examples of press failures: "On one occasion I was described as having 'carried away the green,' and on another I was reported as having 'dropped dead at the hole.'"

The lack of accurate reporting did not stop Vardon from reading the accounts. "I used to go down to the links on the same train as Vardon every morning," wrote one reporter for *Mainly About People*, a popular penny weekly. "He put in his time smoking, and reading the huge New York and other dailies, and it says much for his nerve that he was able to play golf so well after half an hour with American headlines."

Vardon's only defense against the scribes was his manager, Charles Cox. "It was part of his business to try to gorge insatiable would-be interviewers with facts about the champion without letting them approach Vardon, who had not recovered from the effects of the magnificent impudence of the New York interview fiends," reported *Mainly About People*.

CHAPTER 3

The Southern Tour

Head for the Warmth

Vardon spent two more nights in New York City after his Laurence Harbor victory before boarding a train with Charles Cox for the twenty-four-hour trip down the East Coast. Rail travel in America had advanced rapidly in the last two decades of the nineteenth century. Trains served nearly every community in America by 1900, and what was once a dirty, crowded, and uncomfortable means of travel had become luxurious and sophisticated for those of means. George Mortimer Pullman introduced the first sleeping car in 1857, and after some forty years of improvements they were elegantly appointed in beveled glass, inlaid wood, brass fixtures, and rich fabrics. Vardon and Cox spent many hours in Pullman cars, allowing the champion to relax in comfort and arrive relatively refreshed.

Florida was another world for the Englishman. Grand hotels dotted the east coast of the state, luring the wealthy from their estates in the northern metropolitan areas. There were three hotels of note in St. Augustine, and the pros gravitated to the Alcazar, which was known as "the golfers' inn" of the historic town. Directly across the street was the Ponce de Leon hotel.

Golf courses were built to enhance the luxurious lodging, and by 1900 the best professionals were finding not only winter work at the resorts but also an active tournament schedule to keep their competitive skills sharp for the northern tournaments in the season to come. St. Augustine possessed two layouts: the Golf Club, which featured nine holes on the grounds of the ancient fort erected during the Spanish occupation of Florida in the 1600s, and the Country Club, which also served as the headquarters of the Florida East Coast Golf Club Association.

After lunch at the hotel Vardon and Cox adjourned to the Country Club golf links, about three-quarters of a mile distant. According to the *New York Times,* "Both were rather pleased with the appearance of the course, and started at once for a couple of rounds. Vardon drove off easily and only got one over four in the first six holes."

The Alcazar in St. Augustine was known as the golfer's hotel.

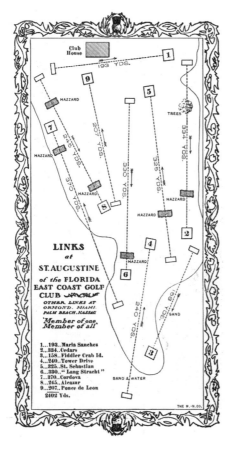

At 2,402 yards, with cross hazards on nearly every hole, the Links at St. Augustine was typical of American golf courses in 1900.

A group of America's best professionals greeted Vardon at St. Augustine, eager to test their skills against the world's best.

Vardon posted 37 on the first circuit of the links, adding a 42 on the second loop.

Dave Findlay was the St. Augustine professional, and many of America's top players were also in attendance. Alex Findlay, Arthur Fenn, George Low, and Bernard Nicholls all came to see Vardon play, and it was decided that Willie Smith, by virtue of being the U.S. Open champion, should play the first match against the visitor.

"With heavy clouds for a start, the day looked anything but promising, but there was a large gallery gathered on the links of the Country Club today," reported the *Times* on February 17. George Low served as Smith's caddie. Fueled by weeks of media coverage, anticipation ran high. "Some thought it would be a walk away, while others thought Smith would put up the best fight of his life with one chance of winning. The crowd was plainly in sympathy with Smith," noted the *Times*.

The U.S. champion got off to a solid start, matching Vardon on the first two holes and taking a 1-up lead on the third. The fourth was an unusual 240-yard par 4. "I must not pass without a word about its unique tee on the top of a tower built of coquina or pulverized shells," wrote John Duncan Dunn in an 1899 article for *Outing*. "As the drive from it is over about 100 yards of water, it is the source of a good deal of fun, although a man who has missed his drive from it may be apt to give it another name."

Willie Smith

Born in Carnoustie to a golfing family, Willie Smith migrated to the States in 1898 and accepted the head professional position at Shinnecock Hills. He joined his brothers Alex and Macdonald in this country and finished fifth in that year's U.S. Open at Myopia Hunt Club. Smith moved to Midlothian Country Club the following year and entered the Open at Baltimore Country Club, where he dominated the field. Posting three of four rounds in the 70s (only ten other rounds below 80 were turned in by the remaining twenty-seven contestants), Smith cruised to an 11-stroke victory. His record stood for 101 years, until Tiger Woods decimated the field at Pebble Beach in 2000, winning by 15. When Alex Smith won the Open in 1906, the Smiths became the only brothers to do so, a distinction that remains today.

By virtue of being the U.S. Open champion, Willie Smith was granted the first game against Vardon.

Smith moved to Mexico in 1907 and served as the first professional at the newly established Mexico City Country Club. Unfortunately his life was cut short in 1915 when he refused to evacuate the clubhouse during the country's revolution. Smith was killed when the building came under rebel attack; he was just forty-one years old.

"Both made long drives from the tower," reported the *Times*. "Vardon reached the green on his second and Smith the far edge. In coming back each missed the hole by a few inches and rolled on. Hole halved in four." Starting on the sixth, Vardon won three holes in a row to wipe out Smith's advantage and take a 2-up lead after nine. Then he caught fire on the second time around.

This time at the tower hole, Vardon unleashed a 225-yard drive, one of the day's longest, "and ran directly over the cup on his iron shot." He won the hole and several others, finishing the morning round 6 up on Smith. A lengthy lunch followed, and play resumed at 3 P.M., although "[t]he weather had turned cold, and wraps of every

The unusual fourth tee was the highest point on the St. Augustine course.

description were in order," wrote the *Times*. "The players had cold fingers, but Smith, at least, was not hampered by the change in the temperature, for he put up a far better game than in the morning, and it looked many times as though he would win out."

Vardon won the first hole of the afternoon installment, going 7 up, and many thought a rout was in the making. Apparently Smith did not share this belief, as his play on the next six holes cut Vardon's lead to 3. "After this Vardon became overanxious. On the eighth Smith drove into the bunker, but was allowed to take his ball out without penalty, and pulled off a half in four," reported the *Times*. The British champion was too much a professional to allow another local rule to affect him, but Vardon was already keeping a mental list of the rules transgressions the Americans relied on to negotiate their links. Partly owing to the newness of many of the courses, but also due to the lack of American talent, the wildness of hazards designed by amateur architects, and the absence of long-standing adherence to a code of conduct that the continental players possessed, nearly every match that Vardon played included a ruling he questioned. In 1900, few golfers in America applied the rules as literally as their British compatriots, and, being raised on the rules, he had difficulty accepting this.

By the time they reached the tower tee for a fourth time, Smith had cut Vardon's lead to three. "The wind was blowing a gale when the men reached the tower for the thirteenth hole. They drove great balls, and Smith made a brilliant approach, but was only able to halve the hole in four," noted the *Times*. Smith never gave up, and

Willie Smith plays from the fair green at the Country Club
in St. Augustine while Vardon looks on.

by winning the fifteenth and sixteenth he delayed the seemingly inevitable outcome until the seventeenth green, where Vardon closed out the match 2 and 1. "It is no disgrace to be beaten by such a man," said Smith in defeat, paying tribute to Vardon's talents. In his first appearance in Florida, Vardon had set a new course record at St. Augustine, taking seventy-one strokes in the morning round, one better than the mark set by George Low a week prior.

A Shocking Headline

Vardon's visit had been preceded by so much hype and speculation it was hard to know exactly how his superior talent would play against the relatively untested American pros. Some thought he would win every match he played; others speculated that the vagaries of golf would inevitably lead to a defeat or two. Just prior to his Florida sojourn, the *Manchester Guardian,* a leading British newspaper of the day, wrote: "The impression is abroad that golfers in America have utterly overrated their own prowess, and that in reality their best game is only a moderately good game. From this point of view Vardon's visit is considered very largely as likely to have a salutary effect, and it is hoped that complete defeat will not prevent them

Ormond was decked in finery for the Vardon visit.

from seeing what a very different thing Vardon's game—and, by implication, the game generally on this side of the Atlantic—is from the one which they are so well content."

It was a short train ride from St. Augustine to Ormond Beach, where the next match was scheduled for February 20. In his tour of Florida resorts, John Duncan Dunn admonished readers thus: "Do not miss Ormond, however, for it is a restful, healthful resort, where you can possess your soul in more patience and enjoy golf free from many of the counter-attractions that impinge so largely upon one's leisure at some of the other resorts." The Ormond Beach Hotel was owned by Henry Flagler and was part of his East Coast chain of luxury palaces.

While the accommodations at Hotel Ormond were beyond reproach, the golf course was vastly different from that at St. Augustine, where the competitors had enjoyed the fact that "the turf is perhaps the best in all the Florida peninsula," according to golf writer W. G. Van Tassel Sutphen.

Ditches, marshes, and railroad tracks were among the many hazards to negotiate at Ormond. But the turf, or lack thereof, was the real issue, according to Sutphen: "The course at Ormond belongs to a hotel company and is kept in as good order as is possible for such a low latitude. And yet the turf is woefully scanty and light-bodied when compared to true sod. The Bermuda grass looks well to the eye, but in reality it is only the next best thing to bare ground. It

The second fairway at Ormond was typical of the condition of the links.

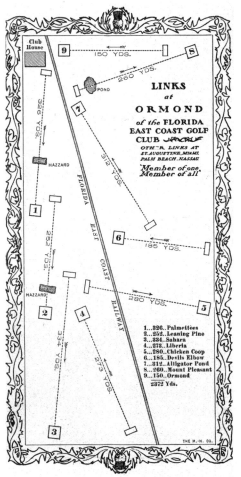

LINKS
at
ORMOND
of the FLORIDA
EAST COAST GOLF
CLUB
OTHER LINKS AT
ST.AUGUSTINE, MIAMI,
PALM BEACH, NASSAU
'Member of one,
Member of all'

Club House

9 ....150 YDS....

8

260 YDS.

POND

7

FLORIDA EAST COAST RAILWAY

312 YDS.

326 YDS.

HAZZARD

1

6 ....185 YDS....

252 YDS.

HAZZARD

280 YDS.

5

2

4

334 YDS.

273 YDS.

3

1...326..Palmettoes
2...252..Leaning Pine
3...334..Sahara
4...273..Liberia
5...280..Chicken Coop
6...185..Devils Elbow
7...312..Alligator Pond
8...260..Mount Pleasant
9...150..Ormond

2372 Yds.

THE M.-N. CO.

The railroad cut through the middle of the newly opened and nearly grassless golf course at Ormond.

has no body (or sole, if you prefer); it lies a tangled mat of creepers, flat on the ground, and, unless carefully trimmed and cut, it makes the most aggravating kind of putting surface, the little loop catching the ball and impeding its progress." Josiah Newman, editor of *Golf* magazine, who was also following the tour, spared no words: "The Ormond course is a desert waste covered with thick little tufts of grass coming up through the sand."

The British *Golf Illustrated* was even more appalled at the conditions. "St. Augustine Country Club grounds are good, and the turf is excellent for this part of the country, but at Ormond it is sand from start to finish, and little roll indeed does the ball get. To further puzzle the newcomer, the greens are of hard clay and as smooth as tables, so a mid-iron approach, just a bit hard, is likely to bound far over the green. On the other hand, a pitched mashie shot, if just a bit short of the green, lands in the soft sand and refuses utterly to roll further."

Vardon issued no complaint about the playing conditions, but after the mud at Laurence Harbor, the piled seashell tees at St. Augustine, and the sand at Ormond, he must have been wondering if there were many "normal" courses in America. On a positive note, the weather had turned tropical, and the match with Bernard Nicholls of the Philadelphia Country Club commenced at 10:30 A.M. under warm sunny skies.

There seemed nothing unusual about the morning eighteen. Vardon went to lunch 4 up, despite a couple of questionable rulings that were in keeping with patterns previously set. On the second hole, Nicholls's approach flew "over the green to the woods. He brought the ball to fair ground without penalty and approached dead," according to the *Chicago Daily Tribune*. It happened again on five when "Nicholls got into the hammock land again, but dropped on fair green without penalty." In between Vardon found trouble as well, but refused free relief despite the suggestion: "Vardon sliced a drive into the woods on the third and gave up the hole without playing."

By the 2 P.M. start of the afternoon round it had turned hot, and Vardon appeared uncomfortable in his woolen outfit. While Nicholls seemed fueled by the warmth, Vardon wilted, and by the time nine holes had been played Vardon's lead had been erased and his opponent stood two ahead. Vardon drove out-of-bounds on the seventh and into a pond on the eighth; then Nicholls enjoyed another favorable drop on the ninth. "Nicholls went into the brush, and as he was allowed to lift without penalty he won the hole in 4 to 6," reported the *Tribune*. Nicholls was also putting extraordinarily well, holing a

Bernard Nicholls

Once Bernard Nicholls beat Harry Vardon at Ormond Beach and later at Brae Burn he achieved a celebrity status that reverberated throughout the golfing world. There is no doubt Nicholls was a competent player. He and his brother Gilbert were raised in England at Folkestone, county of Kent; both served in British clubs before moving to France and then America. Bernard—who later used the shortened Ben—set course records at Deal in England, Cannes in France, and Lenox and Philadelphia in the United States, and he placed seventh in the first U.S. Open he attended.

When the British press questioned his skills and the validity of his win, Nicholls fired off a letter to the editor of *Golf Illustrated* that was published in the May 11, 1900, issue. It read in part:

When Bernard Nicholls beat Vardon he became an instant celebrity in the United States and the United Kingdom.

> On Sunday, February 17, we both left St. Augustine for Ormond, accompanied by a few friends. We both played practice rounds on Monday, the match being at 36 holes on Tuesday, February 19, so our knowledge of the course, as you see, was precisely equal.
>
> In regard to the quality of the course, I'll admit it was not perfect, but the man who says it's the worst in Florida knows very little of what he says, for Vardon himself, with the other professionals, admitted that the greens were the truest they had seen. A glance at Vardon's score in the morning of 72—beating all previous records by four strokes—will show that he was playing almost perfect golf.
>
> A second glance at the score will show that my pace in the afternoon was a hard one to beat, and, although I don't for one moment class myself with Harry Vardon, I would like credit from these narrow-minded reporters for at least one good score in my life.

When he returned to England late in 1900, Nicholls was inundated with offers for challenge matches, although he insisted he was there on holiday. He relented somewhat and defeated Peter Paxton of Tooting but lost to James Braid.

20-footer on the third and "a phenomenal putt of twenty-five yards from the fair green" on six. Nicholls played the nine holes in 34 while Vardon struggled to 42, and then, to the surprise of the crowd, failed to win a single hole the remainder of the match. Nicholls took both the tenth and eleventh, halving the twelfth and thirteenth. "On the fourteenth Vardon foozled his approach and Nicholls scored a great victory by making 5 up and 4 to play," noted the *Tribune,* which clearly had a reporter on the scene who knew little about the correct golf vocabulary.

Vardon's defeat was big news around the country. His being beaten in just the third formal match of the tour was quite unexpected. Those who hoped for a strong American showing cheered; those who didn't offered excuses. "It was true that Nicholls had most of the luck, holing out no fewer than four iron approaches, but Vardon sliced and pulled upon occasions. He had an attack of actual foozles and the result was inevitable," wrote Sutphen. "Nicholls made the third round in 34 strokes, which shows, as plainly as figures can, the essential kindergarten nature of the course," he added.

"The only excuse for Vardon being beaten by Nicholls, that I have heard, is that Vardon had not previously been used to the warm climate in the middle of winter," wrote Newman. "This doesn't do, however, as neither Nicholls nor Smith had passed a winter in Florida previously."

All the scribes seemed surprised that Nicholls had been the one to beat the champion, as his credentials failed to match those of the other American professionals. But *Golf Illustrated* reasoned: "It may be that, like many other distinguished players, he is a much more formidable factor to reckon with in match play than medal play," pointing out that in three appearances in the U.S. Open, Nicholls had failed to finish within four strokes of the winners in any round. They also noted the intimidation factor that Vardon arrived with may have dissipated after his brethren watched him play and realized he was human. "The ordinary run of professionals are usually not in the habit of unearthing their reserve latent talent when first called upon to meet the Champion. It may be that Nicholls is an exception to the ordinary rule however," claimed *Golf Illustrated.* "Vardon nor anyone else could have beaten Nicholls at the game he was playing. A first-class professional, he was more than 'on his game.'"

Vardon seldom made excuses for his substandard play to the American media, quickly realizing that anything he said would be embellished and found on the front page of every paper in America the following day. "There was some excuse for this defeat which I suffered at the hands of Nicholls, who was the only man to defeat me single-handedly throughout my tour," wrote Vardon thirty-three years later in *My Golfing Life.* "Ormond, at this period, was an entirely different course to that which I had been accustomed to play on in this country. There was no grass on the links at Ormond Beach, and it was naturally a very different proposition for me to tackle after having been used to playing from the turf. Anything in the nature of the pitch shot was absolutely impossible there, and it was necessary to cultivate the habit of playing a running up shot for approaches of all lengths."

Scotch, Billiards, and a Laugh

Competitors during the day, the professionals were chums at night—and the Scotch, tobacco, and jokes were dispersed freely. "The professionals while away their evenings playing pool or English billiards," wrote A. J. Coleman. "George Low is the wit of the crowd and the drollest of Scots. Vardon, too, is a joker in his quiet way, and

A coterie of golf professionals played the game during the day and laughed over Scotch and tobacco at night. *Left to right:* Willie Hoare, Harry Vardon, George Low, Willie Smith, G. F. Merritt, Bernard Nicholls.

Palm Beach was the best course the pros played in Florida.

Two holes at Palm Beach were more than 400 yards in length, and both played to a bogey six.

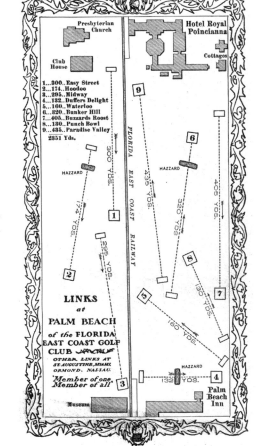

at breakfast one morning reported he had seen Nicholls out in the hall chasing mosquitoes with a niblick."

The next day the entourage continued south, taking up residence at the Royal Poinciana Hotel in Palm Beach. Another magnificent Flagler-owned hotel, the Royal Poinciana and the Palm Beach Inn (renamed The Breakers the following year) accommodated hundreds of well-heeled guests. Poinciana had been built in 1897, the same year a nine-hole golf course was installed, and was said to be the largest wooden structure in the world at the time. In 1901, the Palm Beach Golf Links was expanded to eighteen holes, becoming the first such course in Florida.

"The whole magnificent lawn over which the Palm Beach course runs has had to be coaxed into existence, and to keep it in condition it is piped throughout with a tap every fifty feet," wrote John Duncan Dunn. "The result is a good course, through the greens over the Bermuda grass especially so, but do not attempt to loft onto the putting greens, for if you do your ball will bound off; approach by running up, and then you will discover why, for the place you putt on in Florida is not a green; it is just as gray and hard as a rock."

Although the Palm Beach course featured clay greens akin to Ormond's, the fairways showed considerably more grass. "The course is for the most part good turf," reported the *New York Tribune*, "but the presence of clumps of coconut palms makes accuracy necessary. The sanded clay greens were in excellent shape."

Starting in Florida, and continuing throughout the year, practice matches among the pros consisted of foursomes, or alternate-shot eighteen- and thirty-six-hole events. Vardon and Low teamed up against Fenn and Findlay on February 21, and after fifteen holes Vardon and Low were 2 up—when a rainstorm halted play for the day.

It was estimated that as many as eight hundred spectators turned out for the 10:15 start of the match on a warm and windy holiday to commemorate Washington's Birthday. "A stiff breeze made the air comfortable, but added to the difficulties of driving and putting," noted the *New York Times*. Arthur Fenn was the host pro at Palm Beach, but his buddy Alex Findlay provided the opposition to Vardon. H. M. Forest of Philadelphia caddied for Findlay; Billy Thaw of Pittsburgh carried for Vardon; and A. W. Black of Lakewood acted as referee. After the heat got to him at Ormond, Vardon had discarded the woolen Norfolk jacket, appearing in shirt sleeves and a tie with long pants rather than knickers.

In the heat at Palm Beach, Vardon discarded his flannels
for light summer pants and shirt.

Both players were at the top of their games, and phenomenal putts followed precise approach shots and well-placed drives. When recovery shots were needed the competitors met those challenges as well. Vardon's drive on the tenth finished behind a tree, forcing him to "pick it out with left-handed play." Findlay "got a bad lie in the palms" at eighteen but sliced it out with a brassie and "made a beautiful mashie pitch and fell dead on the green." Meanwhile, "Vardon was on a railroad track, but was successful in holing out in six to seven. The morning play finished even."

Findlay went 1 up early in the afternoon round by winning the fourth, but Vardon captured three of the next five and started the final nine with a two-hole lead. "Findlay sliced his thirteenth drive and fell behind a small shed, but he pitched dead on the green with a beautiful mashie shot, and holed out 3 to 4," reported the *Times*. Vardon lost the one-hole advantage at the following hole, and with only four holes left the match was all square.

But the English champion rallied again on fifteen. "This left Vardon one-up with only two to go, and the excitement intense," reported the *Times*. Findlay captured seventeen, and it all came down to the final hole. Was it possible Vardon could be beaten twice in a row? On the final hole, "[t]he wind sliced Findlay's ball badly and

Alex Findlay

In the first twenty-five years of American golf, few players enjoyed a higher profile than Alex Findlay. Raised in Montrose, Scotland, Findlay emigrated to the United States in the early 1880s to manage a ranch in Nebraska. He laid out a golf course in the northern grasslands and taught the natives to play as early as 1885, moving to Florida to supervise the construction of Florida East Coast Railroad's string of courses in the 1890s.

Findlay was regarded as the premier match-play specialist in the country but shied away from stroke-play events, seldom competing in the U.S. Open and never placing higher than eleventh, in the 1899 contest. Findlay was more of an ambassador of the game and a salesman—promoting the products and services of Wright and Ditson, Spalding, and later Wanamaker's in Philadelphia.

Alex Findlay played more matches against Vardon than anyone during the champion's yearlong tour.

In the first three decades of the twentieth century, Findlay planned more than one hundred layouts in eighteen states—from Maine to Montana, Oklahoma to the Bahamas. Many were built by his three sons: Norman, Ronald, and Richard. His natural style tested the game, while not unduly punishing the less-skilled. Findlay's influence on golf was substantial—ranging from course design to equipment to competition.

he got a bad lie behind the palms again. His brassie carried out, but not in line, and in using it he fell into a bed of oleanders. This cost Findlay the match."

One thing that stood out about the best match of the tour so far was an adherence to the rules of golf. Neither player took a free drop, and the ball was played as it lay through the green. The postgame interviews were unanimous in their praise for the golf that was played; the newspapers called it the greatest match ever played in Florida.

Many thought that the match between Vardon (*left*) and Alex Findlay at Palm Beach was one of the best ever played.

Arthur Fenn

Born in Waterbury, Connecticut, in 1858, Arthur Fenn enjoyed all competitive sports, finding golf to his liking at age thirty-six in 1894. Fenn fashioned a sparkling career as an amateur player, capturing the prestigious Lenox Cup three years running (1895–1897), though never winning the U.S. Amateur in four tries.

In 1897, Fenn turned professional and accepted a job at the Poland Spring House in Maine, where he remained for twenty-five years. His winter post was the Palm Beach Golf Club, a layout he remodeled before installing his daughter as professional to succeed him. While Arthur was considered one of America's first homebred golf professionals, Bessie Fenn was unequivocally the first female golf professional in the country.

Arthur Fenn was America's first homebred golfing talent.

Fenn designed a basic layout in his home town in 1896 and six challenging courses in New Hampshire, as well as a few layouts elsewhere, all before the turn of the century. At the time, he had as much or more artistry in his design than others who were performing similar feats. Little of his work remains, though traces shine through at the Profile Club in Franconia, New Hampshire. Fenn's competitive career as a professional was defined by his matches with Alex Findlay—both as a partner and as an opponent. The two played hundreds of events together over the course of twenty-five years, demonstrating highly skilled golf to thousands of spectators who might otherwise never have seen such.

"I never played a better match," Vardon told the *Tribune,* a sentiment echoed by Findlay: "It was the best match I ever played." All felt they had seen something special, with Smith calling it "one of the best I ever saw," and Low adding, "I don't think a better match was ever played in this country."

The next morning Vardon took on Fenn, and the results were not so dramatic. Fenn only captured two holes in an eighteen-hole match, and one came well after the game had already been decided 6 and 5 in Vardon's favor. In the afternoon a foursome with Vardon and Smith facing Low and Findlay delighted the spectators, ending square after eighteen. An extra nine holes was commenced, finishing in the dark with Vardon and Smith winning 2 and 1.

One final push south brought the golfers to the Hotel Royal Palm in Miami. "Harry Vardon and the party of professional golfers that have been following his matches through Florida reached here late last night," reported the *New York Times* on February 24. Although every Florida stop featured lodging at an elegant hotel of the finest caliber, the Royal Palm was the most memorable. Completed in 1897, the five-story palace measured 680 by 267 feet and included a 40-by 150-foot swimming pool, six-story portico, 578-foot free-standing veranda, and 350 guest rooms, plus another 100 bedrooms for guest support and hotel staff. "Above the rotunda was a look-out platform where every visitor of any consequence went to look at the ocean to the east and the mysterious Everglades to the west. During its heyday the Royal Palm was host to some of the richest and most famous people in the world. The finest private steam yachts tied up at the hotel docks, and the greatest artists were brought to give concerts in the hotel ballroom," wrote society columnist Thelma Peters.

The *Times* described the Miami links thus: "The course is very picturesque, over what was once a savannah. It is skirted by woods

The first tee at Miami.

and its bunkers are stone walls. It is the longest nine-hole course in Florida, being 2,700 yards. The turf is fairly good, but the clay greens are slow at present."

None of the professionals had been this far south before. "As neither Vardon nor George Low, with whom he was scheduled to play a match today, had ever seen the course, it was undecided whether to play it off today or on Monday, but a tossed coin decided, and they started at 10:30," noted the *New York Times.* Low won the first hole with a birdie three, a lead he increased to three by the time they reached the seventh tee. But Vardon reeled off three straight wins to close the first nine all-square. Vardon continued to dominate on the second time around, winning four holes and halving the other five for a lead he never relinquished. He closed out Low on the fifteenth with a 5 and 3 victory.

The professionals stayed for the weekend to enjoy the hospitality at the Hotel Royal Palm and elsewhere in Miami. Although golf courses had been springing up in Florida for a few years, this visit by Vardon and the best professionals in America inaugurated what would become an annual exodus to the winter sunshine and the start of a second season of golf in the south. Competitions and challenge matches were arranged for the pros in the following years, and overseas guests were expected to follow Vardon's lead. The wealthy patrons of golf required such entertainments, though few visitors would exhibit the talent Vardon demonstrated in the winter of 1900.

George Low

George Low was born in Carnoustie, Scotland, in 1874, pursuing there an apprenticeship in golf during the 1890s. He learned all the skills expected of a Scottish professional of his day, including the making and repairing of golf clubs, the keeping of the greens, and the playing of the game.

George Low swings in the typical style of the day.

When the reports of his good friends and fellow natives of Carnoustie, brothers Alex and Willie Smith, filtered back to Scotland about the opportunities available in America, Low followed their lead and made the steamer journey to the United States in 1899. He took a post at Dyker Meadow Golf Club at Fort Hamilton in Brooklyn, New York. "The club is not only one of the most accessible from New York and Brooklyn," wrote Josiah Newman in the *1900 Official Golf Guide*, "but is delightfully situated within full view of the ocean. One or two of the holes are close to the water's edge and there is scarcely a more desirable nine-hole course in the United States."

Low succeeded Mungo Park as professional and greenkeeper at Dyker and made a quick start in professional tournament golf by placing second in the U.S. Open just weeks after his arrival in the country. He later became professional at Ekwanok in Vermont before a long and rewarding stint at Baltusrol in New Jersey. He also designed several golf courses in the early 1900s.

In his later years at Baltusrol, Low invented a furrowed rake that became closely associated with the sand bunkers at Oakmont. The rake prevented bunker escape with the putter, forcing players to show their talents with an explosion shot from the sand. In describing the effect on bunkers Low wrote, "By raking the traps at right angles to the line of play I found that the bunkers maintained a uniform surface much better and for longer periods of time than under the old system of raking them smooth. It was also rarely possible altogether to overcome the penalty."

It is surprising that Low never won the U.S. Open. His second-place finish in his first attempt proved to be his best effort, even though for many years he was never found outside of the top ten.

George Low putts on the third green at Miami.

Plans were made for each of the pros to host Vardon at their northern clubs in the months to come. "The departure of Vardon from Florida has led to an exodus of several other professionals," reported the *Times* on March 8. "George Low, the Dyker Meadow pro, has just returned and will now devote his attention to getting that course in shape for the spring games. Bernard Nicholls, the only man to beat Vardon, returned to his Philadelphia club this week. Smith will remain for a few days at Palm Beach but the end of the month will see him homeward bound. The Florida golf season will practically close this month and on the homeward trip many of the amateurs will stop at Aiken and Richmond for the open tournaments to be held."

Vardon made two stops on his way to Pinehurst for his next highly publicized matches. First he played at the Bon Air Hotel Golf Club, soon to be renamed the Augusta Country Club in Augusta, Georgia, on March 2. For the first time, Vardon beat the best ball of *three* amateurs, Messrs. Cumming, Waller, and Denny, by 6 and 5, posting a course record of 77 in the process. A large crowd attended.

He then visited the Palmetto Club in Aiken, South Carolina, and judging from the scant accounts of the day, it was not his favorite match. Knowing the more-than-cordial southern hospitality exhibited at the fine old club today, Palmetto would probably like nothing more than to have another chance to host Vardon in a more congenial atmosphere. According to the club's own history, "Mr. Vardon, six times winner of the British Open, came to Aiken with the Prince of Wales. Since he was a golf professional, he was denied access to the clubhouse and was not allowed to wear "knickerbockers" on the

The first tee at Bon Air in Augusta, Georgia.

Vardon chips to a sand green at Bon Air while a cow grooms the course in the background.

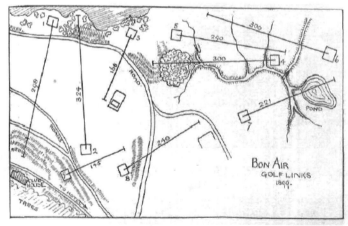

Bon Air in Georgia was renamed Augusta Country Club later in 1900.

Medical Testimonial

"About two months into the trip, on his 'southern swing,' he experienced a product called Bell-cap-sic Plasters, apparently a remedy for 'aches, sprains and strains.' Vardon's testimonial about its medicinal benefits was incorporated into a print ad which introduced to the public at large the concept of the professional golfer extolling the virtues of a product that was not an integral component of the game. The character and perceived reputation of Vardon as a reliable reference source precipitated a breakthrough upon which successive generations of golfers with a public profile would capitalize to their financial benefit."

From *Vardon to Woods: A Pictorial History of Golfers in Advertising* by Alastair Johnston

This advertisement may well be the first endorsement in history of a non-golf product by a golfer.

course—a privilege reserved for gentlemen. He was allowed to smoke during the round by a special dispensation of the golf committee."

Being a *true* gentleman, Vardon made little public mention of his treatment. But the British *Golf Illustrated* could not hold its tongue in an April 6, 1900, article that detailed the courteous treatment he was receiving most places in America. "The exception was at Aiken, in South Carolina, where Vardon was playing the best ball game with two amateurs on the Palmetto Golf Club's course. He was smoking a cigarette during the game, when one of the amateurs accused him of being guilty of discourtesy in doing so. 'At least,' said this eccentric person, 'we might expect as much respect as an amateur would receive on any English course.' Vardon was intensely annoyed, but smoked no more. In the evening, the story having got wind, quite an indignation meeting of golfers was held in the hotel, general sympathy being expressed towards Vardon by everybody."

Vardon didn't let the treatment get in the way of his game. In two eighteen-hole matches he dispensed with the best ball of Jones and Jimmy Mackrell by 1 up in the morning and the best ball of Herbert

The Palmetto Club attracted some of the best golfers from the
Northeast during the winter season.

Leeds and H. R. Johnstone by 9 up in the afternoon. Leeds was off
his game that day but recognized the talent of Vardon, noting that
he "seemed to jump at his ball, when playing for distance, but that
after observing him more closely [I] came to the conclusion, that
it was simply the way in which his arms and feet kept perfect time
with one another."

As for the mysterious mention of the Prince of Wales, no further
data has come to light. After Vardon's treatment at Palmetto, the
British champion caught the next train north—headed for the resort
of Pinehurst.

Golf Greens in 1900

When Vardon turned professional and left Jersey to seek greener pastures
he visited the finer courses of the United Kingdom. From 1893 on, he
played in the Open Championship at such venues as Prestwick, St. George's,
Muirfield, St. Andrews, and Royal Liverpool. These layouts had turf that
had been cultivated for half a century or longer, and although they wouldn't
quite measure up to today's standards of maintenance, they were closer
than one might think.

It was in that decade that Carter's Seeds began to plant golf courses in varieties specifically chosen for the purpose, the result being fabulous stands of turfgrass at such courses as Sunningdale and Walton Heath. But even before that, British courses benefited from well-drained soils and native grasses that thrived when maintained by experienced greenkeepers.

Courses in Britain had been cultivated for decades and featured smooth putting surfaces with well-maintained grass that putted true.

A blend of common bentgrass (*Agrostis vulgaris*), hard or red fescue (*Festuca duriuscula*), and a small percentage of velvet (*Agrostis stolonifera*) formed a luxurious carpet for greens, which were rolled, watered when necessary, and mowed often. The well-drained sandy base yielded predictable incoming approach shots, and the smooth surface resulted in putts that rolled true and quick, especially during important championships.

When greens in America were grassed they were often so shaggy that a golfer's shots on the green were more like chipping than putting.

It's hard to know what Vardon expected of American course conditions as he started his journey, but what he found had to be somewhat of a shock. His first outing at Laurence Harbor Golf Links in Perth Amboy, New Jersey, was played in a mud bowl. The *New York Times* called the conditions "lamentable," and in *My Golfing Life* Vardon noted, "I remember that the clay greens were in such a state that temporary ones had to be made." Drizzle and excessive play had turned the brand-new greens to slop.

From that agronomic debacle Vardon headed to Florida, where he encountered courses devoid of grass. Josiah Newman, editor of *Golf* magazine, wrote: "The Ormond course is a desert waste covered with thick little tufts of grass coming up through the sand." Vardon added that there "was no grass on the links at Ormond Beach, and it was naturally a very different proposition for me to tackle after having been used to playing from the turf."

During his travels Vardon played oiled sand greens at Pinehurst, putting surfaces thinned by winterkill in the White Mountains of New Hampshire, and shaggy carpets soaked by rain in the Midwest. Eventually he discovered some of America's better venues, though even the finest among them had only been tending their greens for seven or eight years. Chicago Golf Club, Shinnecock Hills on Long Island, and the Chevy Chase Club outside of Washington, D.C., showed the English champion there was hope for the future of golf course maintenance in the New World, but he still must have been happy to return to the comfort of British turf for the 1901 season.

Many greens Vardon found on his tour were oiled clay surrounded by weeds—tough surfaces to play a bump-and-run approach to.

Putting on the sand greens he encountered during the first month of his visit was a new experience for Vardon.

CHAPTER 4

North Along the East Coast

In the Sand Hills

"Dear Sir," wrote Harry Vardon to James Tufts at the conclusion of his visit to Pinehurst. "I want to thank you so very much indeed for all the kindness which you have extended to me during my stay at Pinehurst. I have enjoyed playing over your course immensely. It is very sporty, no two holes being alike, the distances are excellent and the hazards well placed, by next season when the new ground becomes thoroughly hardened and the present growth of turf becomes more firmly set, you will have 18 holes which will be a great pleasure to any golfer to play over and in my judgment one which will compare favorably with any of the Eastern courses."

Unlike his treatment at Palmetto, Vardon was once again worshipped as a god from the moment he arrived at the new Pinehurst resort. Here, the patrons and owners of the club were so enamored of the champion that March 9 was designated as Vardon Day in the annals of Pinehurst. Vardon and Cox stayed at the Holly Inn, where they were treated to lavish meals and gracious hospitality conducive to the stellar golf he displayed to the awestruck patrons.

James Tufts had arrived in the Sand Hills of North Carolina just five years earlier. Tufts started as an apprentice in an apothecary, went on to own three pharmacies in the Boston area, and then branched into the manufacture of soda fountains that were installed in drugstores throughout the country. In 1895, he turned the management of his company over to others and purchased five thousand acres of clear-cut timberland in central North Carolina, intent on luring northerners to his sporting outpost. Golf was one of the first amenities he added.

Donald Ross, a name long associated with Pinehurst, had yet to arrive in town, though Vardon would meet him later at Oakley Country Club in Massachusetts. Dr. Leroy Culver, a guest at Pinehurst, had staked out the original nine holes in 1898, and the layout had been expanded to eighteen in January of 1900. It was the first eighteen-hole course Vardon played in America, though it was still

55

The Holly Inn was Vardon's outpost in Pinehurst village.

very primitive compared to the established courses of England and Scotland. Fairways were gang-mowed fields of common Bermuda grass; tees were dirt; greens were round patches of oiled sand; and there was no irrigation of any kind.

After a sumptuous meal, an evening in the smoking room, and a night of good sleep, Vardon was ready for two days of matches at Pinehurst. Friday morning, March 9, 1900, was cold and blustery, and many of the spectators were dressed in overcoats, hats, and gloves. After several weeks of the Florida heat, Vardon was back to his Norfolk jacket and woolen pants and ready to face the best ball of the two Pinehurst professionals: John Dunn Tucker and Lloyd B. Hallock.

"The first drive was made promptly at 10:30, Vardon winning the honor on the toss," reported the *Pinehurst Outlook*. "As he stepped to the tee, the line of spectators (roped off at a suitable distance) carefully watched his every motion. After one or two practice swings, he teed his ball and made a drive of perfect direction. Vardon's second shot brought him within about twenty feet of the hole, from which he putted out, making the hole in 3, against 4 each for his opponents."

Even though Vardon generally swept the ball from the ground, spectators were amazed by the occasional taking of a divot, something the reporter had clearly not seen before. "During his play,

Harry Vardon lines up a putt during his match at Pinehurst.

The practice greens around the clubhouse at Pinehurst in 1900.

many people were seen to examine carefully the spot from which he had just played the ball," noted the *Outlook*. "It would be seen that the ball after contact with his club evidently struck the ground quite hard, leaving an indentation. The effect of this with ordinary players would be to cause the ball to lose a great deal of velocity and consequently its distance, but in Vardon's peculiar way it seemed to have the opposite effect, and gave the ball such a spin that it would always stop dead if striking the green." To nip a shot with bite was apparently unheard-of in Pinehurst circles.

When the morning round was over, Vardon was 2 up on the best ball of the professionals and had set yet another course record. "Vardon's score of 78 lowered the amateur and professional record of the links by three strokes, and considering the fact that he had never seen the grounds before starting to play, proves his wonderful skill and ability," concluded the *Outlook*.

An elegant lunch was concluded in time for a two thirty start. "In the afternoon Vardon played even more brilliantly," reported the *New York Times,* "quickly outdistancing Tucker and Hallock." He went out in 34, and according to the *Times,* "The most brilliant play was that of the seventh, where he brassied beyond the green in two strokes, the length of the hazard being 437 yards. He approached dead and easily holed up in 4." Vardon closed the match on the eleventh by 8 and 7. Playing out his ball he posted 41 for a total of 75, shaving another 3 from the record. "Nearly all his drives on the long holes were 200 yards, several carrying 240 yards." Not bad for a small-headed, nineteenth-century hickory club and a gutty ball.

"To say that the spectators were delighted but expresses it mildly," claimed the *Pinehurst Outlook*. "They were simply carried away with his exhibition, and all realize what a privilege it was to witness his play." Friday night was spent at the Holly, and the entire town of Pinehurst couldn't get enough of their guest. "His modest bearing and quiet demeanor, whether on the links or in the smoking room at the Holly Inn, his gentility and quietness have been remarked upon by all who have come in contact with him," wrote the *Outlook*. "One would naturally look for indications of conceit and appearances of what is commonly called 'the big head,' in a person made such a hero of as Mr. Vardon has been at home and during his visit in this country. Just the reverse is true however, for he avoids public displays and hero worship. The guests of Pinehurst unanimously agree that Mr. Vardon is a modest and unassuming gentleman."

In a pattern that would be repeated throughout his tour, on the second day of play Vardon confronted the two best amateurs of the club. George C. Dutton of Boston held the amateur course record at Pinehurst with an 81; he was partnered with Lathrop E. Baldwin of New York. Saturday was warmer than the previous outing and another large crowd assembled to witness play. Vardon was even better.

In the morning he went out in 33 with only one 5 and the other eight holes equally split between 3s and 4s. He added 38 strokes on the way home for a total of 71, reducing his own course record by another four shots. Before he finished posting another front-nine 33 in the afternoon, the match was already decided in his favor by 12 and 11.

On Sunday, Vardon had another treat for his fans. "He did a little quiet limbering up on Sunday morning, took out his putter, and played six holes with this little club in 22," noted the *Outlook*. Vardon was scheduled to depart on Monday, but there were no other matches scheduled until the weather improved up north. "A number of the gentlemen were so enthusiastic over his play that they could not give him up," reported the *Outlook*. "As a result a purse was raised by some of them for Mr. Vardon to play on Monday. This he very kindly did and again played a beautiful game. His last 9 holes were really the best he played during his stay here, as he came home in 35 and this is even more remarkable than the two 33s he made going out."

Finally, on Tuesday morning, Vardon and Cox boarded the train north, concluding their enjoyable stay at Pinehurst. The paper hinted that Vardon would winter at Pinehurst in future years, suggesting he might move to America and live in Chicago when his tour was over. Of this he had no intent. "Mr. Vardon made many friends during his short stay here, and went away carrying with him the best wishes of this community for a continuation of his phenomenal success on the golf links."

Back to the City

Vardon returned to New York and once again enjoyed the shopping and nightlife of the most active metropolis in the world. Without a match scheduled until March 31, Vardon enjoyed some leisure time and once again visited the Spalding plant in Chicopee, Massachusetts. "Harry Vardon returned to town looking browner and more athletic than ever," wrote the *New York Commercial Advertiser*. "As usual he had little to say and one had to play one's approach shots carefully to get anything out of him. Regarding plans for immediate matches, he has none."

As late as March 27, the identity of his opponent for the next match at Hampton Roads Golf and Country Club in Fort Monroe, Virginia, was up in the air. Willie Dunn, American Open champion in 1894, was scheduled to oppose him, but on March 28, the *New York Times* reported, "Dunn said yesterday that his engagements would prevent him from accepting the invitation." Whether the declination

Willie Dunn Jr.

The Dunn family of Musselburgh made as many contributions to golf as any other British clan. Four sons or grand-sons of Willie Dunn Sr.—Tom, Willie Jr., Seymour, and John Duncan Dunn—designed courses, played professionally, made innovative clubs, and advanced the game in many ways.

Willie Jr. came to America in 1893 as the golf professional at Shinnecock Hills. He won the first U.S. Open at St. Andrew's in 1894, a year before the USGA was formed and officially blessed the event. Based in New York with an office on Fifth Avenue, Dunn taught golf and hobknobbed with celebrities, count-ing among his friends John D. Rocke-feller, W. K. Vanderbilt, Teddy Roosevelt, Buffalo Bill Cody, and Zane Grey. Dunn taught golf to Stewart Maiden—who then, according to Dunn, passed on what he learned to Bobby Jones.

Willie Dunn talked a good game, but got smoked by Vardon ... twice.

Despite the embarrassment of two thrashings by Vardon, Dunn continued to enjoy a high profile in golf for many years, eventually moving to St. Louis and then California—though without national competitive success.

was an attempt at gamesmanship or not, Dunn reversed his decision and played the match. Given the eventual outcome, Dunn would have been wise to keep his original position.

Hampton Roads featured a two-year-old "nine-hole course, very level, with good greens," according to *Harper's 1901 Golf Guide.* "The game had been looked forward to with considerable interest, inas-much as Dunn was one of the few first-class professionals in this country Vardon has not beaten," wrote A. Pottow in *Golf Illustrated.* "Besides this, Dunn quite fancied himself."

Despite the fact they already had a game scheduled for April 10 at Scarsdale, Dunn relented at the last moment and agreed to play Vardon in Virginia, a decision he must have regretted. "The weather was wretched," reported the *Washington Post,* which described "a

Hampton Roads was at the beginning of its second season in 1900.

The Hampton Roads
clubhouse.

piercing northeast wind sweeping across the water and chilling the
spectators, of whom there were probably 500."

Vardon dominated the event, which eventually was suspended
for darkness. "The result was the usual victory for Vardon but on this
occasion by more than the usual margin, the Englishman winning
by 11 up and including the bye holes by 16 up, which is enough to
satisfy the most exacting person," wrote Pottow.

Just about every newspaper in America had been following
Vardon's progress during February and March. The fans in New
York had three daily papers that detailed every match, but his lone
appearance in the metropolitan area had been at Laurence Harbor on

Atlantic City clubhouse and golfing grounds.

Atlantic City Country Club professional John Reid played Vardon in a practice match with a lopsided result.

a miserable day in early February. As April rolled around and the weather improved, New York golfers looked forward to several opportunities to see the champion, the first of which was scheduled not far away in Atlantic City on April 2.

Other than his trip to Garden City when he first arrived—where "we walked around the course, playing a few approach shots," according to his host Josiah Newman of *Golf* magazine—Harry Vardon had yet to see any of America's best courses. The majority of the courses he had played were brand-new, very rough nine-hole layouts designed by amateurs and maintained with limited resources. They were a far cry from the Open rota of championship courses he was familiar with in Great Britain.

Atlantic City Country Club had been established in 1897, and an eighteen-hole course was fashioned by club professional John Reid. This is not the John Reid who established St. Andrew's in Yonkers, New York, and remained a life-long amateur and patron of the game. This Reid arrived from his native Scotland in 1894, represented the Philadelphia Country Club in the first U.S.

The highly anticipated Atlantic City game matched Vardon (*center*) versus the best ball of reigning U.S. Amateur champion Herbert Harriman (*left*) and 1898 U.S. Amateur champion Findlay Douglas.

Open, and held a number of posts at prestigious clubs in the Phila-delphia area. Reid is credited with original designs at Huntingdon Valley Country Club, Riverton Country Club, Wilmington Country Club, Country Club of Scranton, Fox Hill Country Club, and Lancaster Country Club. He was recognized as much for design work that mimicked the courses he grew up on in Scotland as he was for his long driving prowess—a skill he often demonstrated to an astounded public.

The events at Atlantic City took on the aura of a major champion-ship due to three factors: the New York media, his opponents, and the fact Vardon hadn't played much since his success at Pinehurst nearly a month earlier. Vardon was to face the better ball of the reigning U.S. Amateur champion, H. M. Harriman, and the immediate past champion, Findlay Douglas. One paper called it "the most important match ever held in this country," predicting that it "would settle the class of our amateurs compared with those abroad." Expectations were high that our best amateurs could equal the performance dis-played at a similar contest in England, in which the amateur twosome of John Laidlay and Balfour Melville beat Vardon 2 and 1.

Vardon and Cox arrived directly from Hampton Roads a day prior to the match and headed out for a morning round. After getting his

Vardon drove the ball farther than nearly everyone he played against.

Some accounts claimed 2,000 people witnessed the match between Vardon, Harriman, and Douglas at Atlantic City—an enormous crowd for the day.

"distances well in hand," Vardon joined host pro Reid for a second eighteen holes. "The latter (Reid) held the record for the course, 5,770 yards, at 81 strokes," reported the *New York Times*. "But before the last green was reached, Vardon had crushed it as easily as a man does his opera hat." While reducing the course record by 5 strokes on his first attempt was an accomplishment, his 76 was all the more remarkable in that Reid and a group of fine amateur players had never scored under 80, even though they had been playing the layout for more than two years. "The machine-like accuracy of Vardon's game and his record-breaking score have made many of the critics who a few days ago were loudly proclaiming that the amateurs would win,

The day was warm but the wind blew half a gale.

extremely doubtful," added the *Times,* which also noted: "The marked superiority of his opponent evidently took the wind out of Reid, for he could only make 95." That had to be embarrassing.

Some accounts claim that as many as two thousand people came to watch the three golfers on April 3, with many women in attendance as well as all the New York amateur players of note. The day was blustery but warm, with the west wind reported at half a gale in the morning and increasing in the afternoon. The *Boston Daily Globe* deemed it "the best golf ever seen in the United States," but among the amateurs, "especially did Douglas distinguish himself. Herbert Harriman played brilliantly at times and like a novice at others."

Vardon appeared in his dull green Norfolk jacket and knickerbockers, seemingly unaffected by the large and enthusiastic crowd. "The committee was forced to hold back the eager crowd with long ropes, behind which men and women stood five and six deep," reported the *Times.* "The shots being made, this line of expectant humanity moved forward 100 yards or so, stopped a minute or two, then on again, in this way going twice over the long course, a walk of full seven miles for those who watched the entire 36 holes. A larger or more enthusiastic gathering could not be seen at a National championship."

Vardon was on his game despite the "wind blowing a mild hurricane in his face" on some holes. The amateurs stayed with him on the first nine holes, falling only 2 down. But Vardon posted 77 after eighteen for a 4-up tally and rapidly added to the margin in the afternoon. Another 38 on the front nine doubled his lead, and he closed out his opponents on the tenth by 9 and 8.

Herbert Harriman and Findlay Douglas

When Harriman won the U.S. Amateur in 1899, he was the first native-born player to do so, knocking out both the favorites—Charles Blair Macdonald in the semifinal and defending champion Findlay Douglas in the final—to capture the trophy. Harriman was the consummate amateur, circulating in the finest circles of New York and Newport without financial constraints.

Born in St. Andrews, Scotland, Douglas captained the University golf team before moving to America and winning the 1898 U.S. Amateur. Douglas was a long driver as a youth and remained a consistent player throughout his life, winning senior titles into the 1930s.

Findlay Douglas and Herbert Harriman.

On this day his game was superior to those of America's best amateurs on all fronts, but the distance he hit the ball was a revelation to Reid and everyone else in attendance, including the *Times* reporter. "Playing the long fifth Vardon cleared the bunker, 475 yards from the tee, in 2, getting the almost phenomenal distance of 485 yards in two shots. After this Vardon walked away from his foes fast and triumphantly. He won five holes in succession."

The British magazine *Golf Illustrated* couldn't help but declare that "Vardon's victory over the best ball of Messrs. Herbert Harriman and Findlay Douglas by 9 up and 8 to play in 36 holes, hardly bears out the idea that American amateur play is equal to ours."

"American Rules"

Yet four days later, Vardon was defeated by two amateurs—college students at that—in what was deemed a "practice match." After two nights back in New York, Vardon and Cox traveled to the New

Vardon was beaten by young Yale golfers in a practice match at
New Haven Country Club.

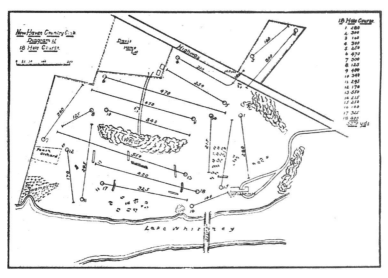

Vardon won both of his official matches on the eighteen-hole
New Haven course.

Haven Golf Club in Connecticut. The course had been designed by
transplanted Scot Robert Pryde, one of the earliest course designers in America who had a talent for the practice. Pryde followed the

Vardon match, leaving the playing to the younger set, but later, in a lecture about early golf in New Haven, he had this observation on the clubs Vardon played with: "When Harry Vardon came here in 1900 his clubs were short with very small heads. They were copied here and made by A.G. Spalding and Bros., and there was a great run on the Harry Vardon Clubs; naturally being shorter they were more accurate to hit with. Each one thought that the clubs used by such a good player would be the right thing for them, with the result that the clubs were in general use for some years." How Vardon played so magnificently with short clubs, and sometimes choked up on them as much as three inches, is a mystery.

The opponents for his practice match were Thomas L. Cheney of South Manchester, Connecticut, the champion of Connecticut and Yale, and T. Markoe Robertson of New York City, the captain of the Yale golf team. A large crowd was reported, coming from all the clubs of the state. The amateurs walked away with the controversial victory 3 up after eighteen holes.

Robert Pryde

Born in 1870, Pryde grew up near St. Andrews before embarking upon his schooling in Dundee and at the Technical College of Glasgow. He came to the United States in 1892 after a clubmaking apprenticeship, taking a job as a cabinetmaker in New Haven, Connecticut. In 1895, he was persuaded to construct a golf course for staff and students at Yale University, and so began a fifty-year career in the game. Though his first design eventually went out of existence, Pryde went on to plan a half dozen other layouts in Connecticut, serve as the secretary-treasurer to the Connecticut State Golf Association (CSGA) for twenty-three years, and patent several golf devices of merit. He also coached the Yale golf team, wrote and lectured on the game, and established the Connecticut Men's Open in 1931. To this day, the CSGA Connecticut Amateur trophy is awarded in his name.

Robert Pryde designed the New Haven Golf Club course and several other early Connecticut courses.

Early in the match, a misunderstanding of the local rules angered Vardon, and the champion almost stopped the match mid-way through. While both sides blamed the other, and although Vardon experienced many inaccurate quotations in American newspapers during the tour, this one from Albert H. Barclay, the reporter from the *Boston Daily Globe,* seems pretty difficult to misinterpret: "After the match he [Vardon] said to me, 'I have had the same experience at every course that I have played over in this country, with the single exception of that at Atlantic City. You Americans don't play golf. You do not know the rules. There is only one way to play, and that is according to the rules of the game. It is ridiculous to have adjustable rules for different courses. A hazard should always be a hazard. This morning when I went over the course I was told that the rules were one thing and this afternoon I was told that they were another, but I stuck to the rules."

The next day, Vardon played two eighteen-hole "official matches," against Yale golf team members—taking on A. T. Dwight Jr. of Dyker Meadow and L. P. Myers in the morning, and Charles Hitchcock Jr. of Point Judith and Eben M. Byers in the afternoon. The morning contest was close. Even though Myers shot 86 and Dwight 97, their best ball was 82, just three off Vardon's 79. But the champion caught fire in the afternoon, lowered the course record from 75 to 71, and beat the best ball of Hitchcock and Byers by eight strokes. Afterward he praised the course and said, "The greens are by far the best that I have found in this country."

Vardon and Cox returned to New York, awaiting a rematch with Willie Dunn at the Scarsdale Golf Club. Dunn had been humiliated by Vardon two weeks earlier at Hampton Roads, but the weather

One of the best Yale golfers in 1900, E. M. Byers went on to win the U.S. Amateur in 1906.

Amateur Charles Hitchcock Jr. teamed with Byers in an afternoon match against Vardon at New Haven Golf Club.

had been challenging and the course unknown. The boastful Dunn still believed he had a chance against the English champion on friendly grounds, and Scarsdale was quite familiar to Dunn. He had designed the 2,697-yard, nine-hole course two years earlier, a course that included a par 4 that crossed a four-acre lake on both the drive and approach shots.

About five hundred spectators assembled for the contest, including all the top amateurs of the region. "Nearly all of the metropolitan clubs had representatives at the links," wrote the *New York Times,* and John Reid Sr. of St. Andrew's acted as "umpire of the match." The links were laid upon a series of knolls and plateaus; as the *Times* put it, "The Scarsdale golf course is a picturesque study in Westchester County kopjes." (Kopje is an Afrikaans term for a small, flat-topped hill or butte.) Some tee balls required a substantial carry to the next kopje, and failure to attain it could result in a grave lie at the base of the upsweep. Scarsdale replaced this layout with an eighteen-hole course later in 1900, but at the time of this event it was yet another substandard track along Vardon's trail. "The greens, with the exception of the eighth, situated in a well-turfed hollow, were not in condition to insure anything near perfection in the putting line," reported the *Times.*

Vardon wasted no time in moving ahead of his opponent, taking three of the first four holes. If it hadn't been for some timely putting, Dunn might have been more than eight down after the morning eighteen. "Dunn's specialty in the match lay in a few sensationally brilliant putts, while Vardon was beautifully steady throughout, and gave many an illustration of the power he can put into a drive and the distance he can get." To the amazement of the crowd, Vardon consistently drove the ball more than 200 yards and closed out Dunn on the eighth green of the afternoon play. "Whatever was the reason, Dunn did not show the game that some of the spectators had seen him play two or three years ago," noted the *Times.*

Whereas most of the courses Vardon played were on level sites,
Scarsdale featured holes with considerable movement.

The "kopjes" of Scarsdale.

Carries like this one at Scarsdale were intimidating, even for the
golf professionals of the day.

After the match Dunn was quoted by *Golf Illustrated* as saying: "Vardon plays the wrong way, his grip is wrong, and he has not a good swing." Surprising words from a man who had been beaten by 11 and 10 initially, and 12 and 11 in the rematch.

Vardon's first appearance in the Boston area was widely anticipated. George Wright was the father of golf in the region and had been extolling the game's virtues since 1890. He was instrumental in arranging Vardon's tour, suggesting his sponsorship to Spalding, the company that had purchased Wright's own Wright and Ditson Sporting Goods. Wright was a member at the Wollaston Golf Club and was determined to have Vardon on his home links. "It is not expected that he would play any matches in the neighborhood of Boston on the present trip," the *Boston Evening Transcript* wrote of Vardon, "but the membership of the Wollaston Club, with characteristic enterprise, hastily made arrangements to have him play on their links before he goes to England, feeling that Vardon may not return to this country after their championship, and that if he should, it would be much more difficult to secure him."

Wollaston was in the process of adding nine holes to their course, but the match was scheduled for April 18 on the original nine, and Vardon's customary fee of $250 was offset by an admission charge of one dollar per person. A. Linde Fowler, the premier golf writer in New England at the time, wrote, "That was the first instance, in my ken, where admission was charged for a golf match in this district." Given that Fowler described the weather as "execrable" and "one of Wollaston's windiest early season days, raw in the bargain," it was a wonder anyone attended.

Vardon struggled through two 18-hole matches, braving the elements on a miserable day, typical of coastal New England at that time of year. In the morning he played the best ball of professional Robert Stronner and Arthur Fenn, beating them 3 and 2. His driving, approach shots, recovery skills, and putting were superior to those of his opponents. The newspapers were filled with copy such as "How does Vardon reach the consummate skill which puts him almost alone in the golf world? How does he accomplish the strokes which have made him dominate the golfers of the old world?" The answers involved long, precise explanations of where his feet were positioned, what his follow-through entailed, and how his grip differed from his contemporaries. The golfer himself offered a simpler explanation: "The essential point of Vardon's play is, as he says, to get the ball where he wishes it to go," reported the *Boston Daily Globe*.

Indoor Exhibition

In conjunction with his visit to the Boston area, Vardon was asked to appear at the Jordan Marsh store and demonstrate his techniques of driving a golf ball. A net was set up with a putting green nearby, and, of course, "There will be a large assortment of his clubs in the golf department," reported the *Boston Daily Globe*. It was also advertised that Mr. Vardon would be prepared to answer questions about the particulars of his style. Vardon was expected to hit balls for half an hour, take a similar break, and then resume his demonstration from 9:30 A.M. until 5 P.M.

"I would not have accepted this offer in the ordinary way as I was giving sufficient exhibitions out of doors," wrote Vardon. "The reward, however, was of such splendid proportions it would have been ridiculous to refuse it."

When Vardon arrived on the fourth floor of the store, "There were several hundreds of people present when I made my first appearance, and, at the end of the allotted time, I retired in accordance with the programme. To my great astonishment the spectators broke into thunderous applause, clapping and cheering in such a way that I was forced to reappear."

Every time Vardon tried to take a break the cheering forced him back to the tee, and as new people arrived it was harder and harder to step aside. "To me it was difficult to understand what anyone could see in this performance, as hitting ball after ball into a net did not strike me as anything very thrilling to watch." Eventually, to relieve the boredom, Vardon played some mashie shots, aiming at a metal object on the ceiling. "I had just hit one of these taps when the manager came rushing into the store and asked me to stop. He promptly explained that if I struck and thereby turned on one of the taps which connected with the fire extinguisher, the store would be flooded."

HOW HE DOES IT.

Exhibition by Vardon, the Champion Golfer.

Crowds Watch Him at Store of Jordan, Marsh & Co.

Methods He Uses to Get His Wonderful Distance.

His Easy Swing and Perfect Timing the Secret.

Extraordinary Accuracy in Half Shots and Putting.

On the top floor of Jordan, Marsh & Co's store, yesterday morning and afternoon, Harry Vardon, the champion golfer of the world, gave exhibitions of the methods he uses in making the strokes which have given him his unique place in the world of golf.

ADDRESSING THE BALL.

Portion of a longer article in the *Boston Daily Globe*, April 18, 1900.

At his next break, Vardon said he "fled from the building as fast as possible," though no one seemed to notice that he cut the exhibition short by an hour. In an April 18, 1900, article the *Boston Globe* raved about the demonstration, how precise Vardon was, how clearly he described his motions, and how direct he was in answering questions, especially those posed by the large number of women in attendance. It comes as no surprise that the store completely sold out of Spalding golf clubs.

The afternoon train brought many more spectators to the club and the team of Wollaston amateur Clifton L. Bremer and Alex Campbell, professional at The Country Club, to challenge the champion. The course was soggy, the wind was howling, Vardon was tired, and his opponents were motivated. By the third hole the best ball was 2 up on the Englishman, a margin they maintained at the turn.

Bremer had carried the home team on the front nine, but Campbell came to life on the back. Neither could outdrive Vardon, but precise iron play and good putting kept the match square until the twelfth, when Vardon knocked a mashie within ten feet of the hole, converted the birdie, and took a 1-up lead—his first of the match. But Bremer made the only four on the sixteenth and squared the contest, which is where they stood at the final teeing ground. "Vardon lined out a long drive and all three were on the green in two," stated the *Globe*. "Bremer was short on his putt six feet and he failed to hole. Campbell's putt was short a foot and Vardon had two for the hole. Vardon putted out, winning the match by one, after one of the most interesting and plucky contests in which the champion ever has played."

Five More Matches and Home

After having been beaten by Bernard Nicholls in Florida, Vardon agreed to a return match with the Philadelphia Country Club professional. But by the time Vardon arrived at that club two months later, Nicholls had moved to Boston to join his brother Gilbert in a golf shop business. The Club at Bala felt it had two worthy opponents to replace Nicholls, one of them Willie Thompson, who had defeated Nicholls by 9 up in a thirty-six-hole match. Thompson was partnered with Harry Gullane, who had placed third in a long driving contest at the 1899 U.S. Open.

Alex "Nipper" Campbell

One of six golfing brothers, Campbell was among the most colorful figures in early American golf. He grew up in Troon, where he captured the Scottish National championship at the age of fifteen, and came to America in 1899 as the golf professional at The Country Club in Brookline, Massachusetts.

Only five feet, five inches tall and "stocky and cocky," the Nipper never lost his thick Scottish brogue and sharp wit, offering advice to his pupils such as, "Swing the clubhead. If y'have the swing, y'can git along with a potato and a hoe handle in this game." He explained to reporters his teaching theory: "Man's like a narrow-moothed whiskey bottle. He can only taka word or two at a gulp. Ye have to tak it slow."

Alexander "Nipper" Campbell was a colorful character and one of five Campbell brothers who advanced American golf in the early years of the twentieth century.

A crafty shotmaker, Campbell could play the game with aplomb, repeatedly finishing in the top twenty in the U.S. Open for nearly two decades, with a third in 1907 his best result.

A finely maintained green at Philadelphia Country Club.

Vardon putting at the Philadelphia
Country Club.

Gullane was the first pro to regularly outdrive Vardon from the tee. "Vardon was not a little disappointing at several stages of the match," reported the *Boston Daily Globe*. "His driving was for the most part good, but on several occasions Gullane led him from the tee by anywhere from 20 to 30 yards." Vardon could compensate for that disadvantage with precise second shots, but it was his performance around the green that nearly cost him the match.

The *Globe* called it "erratic," adding: "On several occasions he putted like a novice, as, for instance, when he drove the seventh green, within a yard of the hole, then took three putts before finding the cup." A three-putt from three feet—what could be next? "He followed this up at the next hole by missing an eight-inch putt for a half."

The game was a tight one, and after eighteen holes Vardon was 1 up in match play, though down by a stroke if the score were tallied in medal play. "When all is said and done, however, it must be admitted that Vardon played like the race horse he undoubtedly is. When called upon for a supreme effort he responded in championship style, and with a splendid in-journey of 36 he won the match practically on the wire." His 156 for the two rounds was four strokes better than the best ball, but his match-play victory margin a scant 1 up after thirty-six.

It must be remembered that although he was being the best golfer on the planet, Vardon was still considered a working-class laborer by the social elite at America's best private clubs. Decades later the Scarsdale club history book referred (with incorrect spelling) to the champion as Harry Varden, and the Philadelphia Country Club history made the same mistake and dismissed his visit in one sentence,

Vardon putts at Oakland Golf Club on Long Island
while Walter Travis looks on.

stating: "And sometime during the preceding year, Harry Varden gave a golfing exhibition on the Club course."

Three days after Philadelphia it was on to the Oakland Golf Club near Bayside on New York's Long Island and their 3,010-yard course—one of the longest in the country. Before he moved to Garden City later in 1900, Oakland had been Walter Travis's home club. He had learned his golf there, and although his national titles were still in the future he had already tasted considerable regional success. Travis was fascinated by Vardon; he had followed him at both Laurence Harbor and Atlantic City and was instrumental in persuading Oakland to pay the champion's fee for an appearance. "Oakland has concluded to have Vardon out probably next week, if it can be arranged, to play either Findlay Douglas and myself or Jamie Douglas, our professional and me," Travis wrote to his fiancée, Nan.

Professional Douglas got the nod on April 24 and then a not-very-favorable review in the *Boston Globe:* "Travis was a little off his game, and Douglas, while at times playing brilliantly, was very erratic." But the paper went on to say, "Probably no match which has been played in this country was ever watched by such a congregation of expert men and women golfers as was today's."

Walter Travis

Born in Australia in 1862 and naturalized as an American citizen shortly after his arrival in New York in 1886, Walter Travis was one of the most important figures in American golf in the first three decades of the 1900s. In addition to being a prolific writer and the founder and editor of the *American Golfer* magazine, Travis was a fierce competitor, winning the U.S. Amateur three times and the British Amateur in 1904—the first non-British player to win the coveted title. When his playing days were over, Travis turned his attention to golf course architecture, designing some twenty-five golf courses, primarily along the East Coast.

Walter Travis and Harry Vardon became friends during his visit, a relationship that blossomed when Travis visited the United Kingdom in 1904.

In 1900, Travis was on the edge of his breakthrough, having enjoyed considerable local success in the New York area. Travis studied Vardon's technique and demeanor, and the two developed a mutual admiration that lasted for decades. They played together when Travis visited England in 1904 and renewed their friendship on Vardon's two subsequent trips to America in 1913 and 1920.

The *New York Times* headlined its article "Easy Victory for Vardon," told of his 6-and-5 win, and reported that his long game neared perfection. It's amusing that Travis, who could recount every stroke of his triumphs, claimed not to remember the score when writing an autobiography for *American Golfer* magazine twenty-six years later. Travis did recall, however, many other details worth reproducing.

"In 1900 Harry Vardon played an exhibition match at Oakland against the better ball of myself and James Douglas, the local pro. I know we got the worst of it, but I do not recall definitely by what margin. Vardon did a 76. A little later I had the satisfaction of beating this record by one stroke.

"Vardon at that time was playing with wooden clubs with quite small heads of dogwood, with leather faces and rather limber shafts,

Pro James Douglas (*left*) and Travis admire Vardon's driving technique.

Vardon at the finish of an approach shot
while the Oakland patrons look on.

and some of his shots were a revelation to most of us in respect of distance. I recall one in particular, a brassie second on the old sixth hole, which carried into a cross bunker that even the youngest of us were glad to get over with our thirds. It was fully 225 yards, all carry—as were all his wooden shots.

The famous "Heavenly Twins" hole at Oakland.

"Then, again, while we were all well satisfied to negotiate the 'Heavenly Twins' with two full wooden shots, Vardon easily got home with a cleek and an iron. The ball then in use was of course a guttie, 27 dwts.—very much on the light side compared with the present day ball of fully 31 dwts. Light as they were they were harder to get up than their more modern compeers.

"This lack of weight operated unfavorably in a heavy wind, especially in the case of the all-carry wooden shots that characterized Vardon's play. A notable illustration of this was shown in his match against the better ball of Findlay Douglas and Herbert Harriman at Atlantic City the same year. Mr. H. C. Fownes measured all of Vardon's tee shots and the longest was 142 yards!"

It's amazing that Vardon could outdistance nearly everyone he played against, given the lack of ball flight in the wind and his use of small-headed clubs, made with dogwood and faced in hard leather. Travis and Vardon would play together again when Travis prepared for the 1904 British Amateur in England, as Vardon was one of the few golfers in the United Kingdom who warmly welcomed Travis on his famous winning trip.

Vardon's next match was arranged for the Allegheny Country Club in Pittsburgh. The club had been established in 1895 and for the first few seasons featured a six-hole course that was extended to nine prior to the Vardon visit. Later that year the club moved to Sewickley. In his thirty-six-hole match against Alex Findlay, Vardon tied the six-hole record of 33, but over the new course of nine holes. For the original six holes he scored 22. Vardon dusted Findlay 11 and 10.

The Allegheny clubhouse when the club was still in Pittsburgh.

A difficult tee shot at Allegheny.

Vardon returned to New York for his next encounter. Dyker Meadow Golf Club had been founded in 1895 on part of what is now Dyker Beach Park, and George Low was the pro/greenkeeper. The course was located in Fort Hamilton, off Seventh Avenue and Ninety-Second Street, at the southwest corner of the park. Tom

Tom Bendelow

One of the true pioneers in American golf, Thomas Bendelow arrived in America in 1892 and took a job setting type for the *New York Herald*. His move to golf came quite by accident, after he answered an ad for a golf instructor placed in the newspaper he worked for. By 1895 he was designing courses for wealthy clients, and shortly afterward he joined the Spalding Company.

Over the years with Spalding he gave golfing demonstrations, laid out hundreds of golf courses in every part of the country, wrote extensively about the game, and edited the annual *Spalding Golf Guide*. Bendelow also was an instrumental part of Vardon's trip, helping to manage his travel, deal with the media, play as his partner when called upon, and serve as a caddie. In that role at the 1900 U.S. Open, Bendelow made a contribution to Vardon's success that the Englishman always remembered.

Bendelow, an employee of Spalding, was the course designer, and *Harper's Golf Guide* called it the "best nine-hole course in the United States." The layout traversed naturally undulating ground, skirting two ponds and playing along the beach at Gravesend Bay, "with very good turf and excellent greens and many artificial hazards."

It was speculated that Low, runner-up in the previous U.S. Open, would give Vardon a good match, "as Low knows every blade of grass there, and will have a decided advantage," according to *Golf Illustrated*. Low had already faced Vardon in Florida, so whatever butterflies he felt had long been put to rest. Vardon familiarized himself with the layout in a practice match on May 1. Partnered with green chairman W. B. Crittenden, Vardon opposed host pro Low and Dyker president Daniel Chauncey in a best-ball foursome. Vardon and Crittenden were 4 up after nine and easily won the match by that margin after all eighteen were completed.

The next day was conducive to good golf, and a crowd of 1,200 assembled to watch the proceedings. "If the glory of winning big golf matches amid the plaudits of enthusiasts has not become monotonous to Harry Vardon, then he must have enjoyed his triumph yesterday over the Dyker Meadow professional George Low," noted the *New York Times*.

"Low began the morning round as he did about two months ago in Florida, by taking the lead," continued the *Times*. "For the first nine holes he was Vardon's equal. The latter excelled in his long shots, while Low was marvelously steady on the green." Low built a two-hole lead after the first nine but squandered it quickly, end-

Dyker Meadow was one of the foremost clubs in the
New York metropolitan area.

ing the morning round 3 down with 43 to Vardon's 37. "In the afternoon Vardon simply walked away from his opponent. He finished the first nine holes in 36, equaling the record once made by Low." His afternoon 73 was a new eighteen-hole record, eclipsing Low's old mark of 77.

With the Open Championship scheduled for June 6 and 7 at St. Andrews, and a crossing of the Atlantic involving seven to ten days at sea, Vardon hesitated to schedule many matches for May. He needed a trip home and time to prepare for the championship, so many thought his match at Dyker Meadow would be the last of this portion of the tour. But immediately after the game, Vardon and Cox boarded the overnight train to Providence, Rhode Island, and a May 3 date at Wannamoisett Country Club.

George Low started his American career at Dyker Meadow in 1899 before settling in for a lengthy tenure at Baltusrol in New Jersey.

Wannamoisett had inaugurated play in 1899 on nine holes designed by Willie Campbell. At 2,839 yards the course could offer a stiff test when the wind was up, and without much tree cover in those days, the wind was up often. Vardon caught the worst kind of early May day by the ocean: cold, wet, and windy. One of the *Boston*

WANNAMOISETT GOLF CLUB.

Opponent ....

Date ....

Bog.	Yds.	H'l	NAMES.	Self	Opp.	Hole	Self	Opp.
5	427	1	Topper's Trouble			10		
6	525	2	Pilgrim's Progress			11		
4	280	3	Polo			12		
5	316	4	Colonel's Pocket			13		
4	270	5	Robin Lane			14		
4	225	6	Four Oaks			15		
5	311	7	Quarry			16		
4	225	8	Twins			17		
4	280	9	Home			18		
41	2839		Total					

E. A. JOHNSON & COMPANY, PRINTERS, 87 WEYBOSSET STREET, PROVIDENCE, R. I. TELEPHONE.		
First Nine Holes		
Gross Total . .		
Handicap		
Net Total . . .		

The scorecard from Wannamoisett in 1900.

Globe's subheads read, "In Morning Champion Plays in Heavy Storm." The article related how "Harry Vardon, the English golf champion, came here today and in a downpour of rain, with a Northeast breeze, he beat the best ball of W. D. Brownell and D. J. Sully by 8 up, 18 holes."

That Vardon could take the overnight train, jump out on a course he had never seen before in a raging storm, and beat the club's two best amateurs so handily was unlike anything the brave patrons who endured the deluge had seen before. "The storm was so severe in the morning that Vardon's play was extraordinary," claimed the *Globe*. "Clubs were wet, players were drenched and chilled by the rain, casual water lay all over the course, and the grass was heavy with water. It was difficult to tee a ball the wind was so strong. Vardon's play was a revelation to the spectators."

Vardon managed an 82 in the gale, while his opponents posted 93 and 99. During lunch the rain stopped and the skies cleared a bit, but Vardon never warmed up. The afternoon was as much a surprise as the morning but for a different reason. "It was an eighteen-hole affair on a soggy course, but with otherwise perfect conditions," wrote the *New York Times,* "and the British champion went down before the best ball of two amateurs by a score of 2 up and 1 to play."

C. L. Bremer of Wollaston, who had barely lost to Vardon two weeks earlier, replaced Sully as Brownell's partner in the afternoon. "In the afternoon Vardon, while playing his usual sure, steady, and at times brilliant game, could make little headway against the great team work of his opponents," reported the *Times*. "He frankly admitted that the result was perfectly fair and unquestioned."

Brownell and Bremer both beat Vardon on the first hole of the match—perhaps a sign of things to come. He squared it at the second but lost the third and never tasted the lead again. After nine he was two in arrears, but he fought back in the early going on the second loop. When he won the sixteenth he was only one down with two to play and those in attendance expected the amateurs to

The first hole at Wannamoisett was aptly named "Topper's Trouble" and featured a drive over a pond.

fold in the final battles. The seventeenth hole of the match was Wannamoisett's eighth: a 225-yard, bogey-4 named "Twins." Vardon was on in two while Bremer was still 30 yards out as he ran his pitch shot toward the hole. The ball struck the flagstick and disappeared into the cup for a three, and when Vardon failed to make his putt to tie, the match was over. The young Harvard graduates had handed Vardon his third defeat in twenty-six matches—an enviable record but a sour ending. Two days later he was on his way back to England.

W. D. Brownell teamed with another amateur to defeat Vardon at Wannamoisett.

CHAPTER 5

The Former

Home for the Open

Before he left for England, Vardon was interviewed by the *New York Times* and the *Boston Daily Globe*. "I've had the best time of my life in America," he told the *Daily Globe*. "I am charmed with Americans. I used to have some exaggerated ideas of this country and the people. But I shall never have a word against Americans again. They are the nicest lot of people I ever met. Your women; they are the best lookers in the world."

With a little gamesmanship Vardon downplayed his chances at the Open Championship. "I don't expect to win. The course at St. Andrews doesn't suit me. I am up against 20 men who know every blade of grass on the links."

When asked if he was taking his Spalding clubs back with him, like a seasoned spokesperson, he plugged the sponsor. "I couldn't go back without them. I never saw any clubs as well finished or as well made as the American clubs."

The man clearly had a proclivity for good public relations. Despite having played on some awful courses, Vardon singled out for the *New York Times* the good ones he had seen: "Some of your courses are much better than I had been led to believe. I can only talk of those I have seen, but Atlantic City, Garden City, Oakland, Dyker Meadow, and the Philadelphia Country Club are all worthy of being called excellent courses. The best putting greens I played over are those at Oakland and the Wannamoisett course of Providence."

There was one more morsel for his audience before he left. "Several of your younger golfers are developing genuine talent and are playing with a care for the best style. In this class I should place R. C. Watson Jr., Harry Hollins, John Reid Jr., T. M. Robertson, and C. M. Meyers." And with that the dashing champion was gone; headed for home aboard the ocean liner *Lucania*.

Upon docking Vardon returned to Ganton, where he was reunited with his wife Jessie. Before he left for America, Vardon had arranged for Jessie's sister Annie to move to Ganton from Jersey and keep her

Thoughts on Practice

Few professionals of 1900 spent a great deal of time on the practice range or in the gym. Beating balls and lifting weights are modern responses to substandard play; the champions of old just headed out for another round. When he first arrived in America Vardon said, "I never train. It won't do. It makes you nervous. I sometimes stay up all night before a tournament."

During his tour Vardon showed he hadn't changed his mind at all when he wrote, "I am often asked how I train for big matches. I always reply, 'I don't train at all, and the more you train the worse golf you'll play.' Of course a man must keep himself fit, but I do not alter my ordinary life before a big match or competition. I am neither an abstainer nor a non-smoker. Indeed, I am a heavy smoker, and if I don't smoke when playing, it is only because the spectators might think it disrespectful, or that I was not trying my hardest. Certainly it is not because I think it would in any way injure my play."

company. This wise step had ensured Jessie's happiness for the year, and the sisters were living comfortably thanks to the financial results of Harry's passion and talent for golf. His wife was in her best spirits since their wedding nine years earlier.

Vardon had a couple of weeks to prepare for the Open, and he did so in his preferred fashion, relaxing and playing casual matches at Ganton. En route to the Open on June 1, he played Musselburgh and lowered the course record from 70 to 67, leaving little doubt he was ready to defend his title.

Vardon and J. H. Taylor matched 79s in the opening round at St. Andrews, but that's as close as Vardon would get to his friendly adversary. He finished second, but eight shots distant, as Taylor saved the best round of the entire tournament for his last—a 75.

The British press was brutal, taking every chance it could to blame the loss on the ruination of Vardon's game by the inferior courses he was forced to play in America. "We are afraid Vardon's toilsome experience over primitive American links is chiefly responsible for his loss of form on the true courses of this country," wrote the *Yorkshire Daily Post*, "and as he is about to return for another three months' tour he will not have much chance of recovering it."

But *Country Life* had it right. "It is rather amusing to read the accounts in some of the papers. They say that his American tour has upset his game a little. Vardon played an uncommonly fine game, as good a game as even his grand play before he went to America. The real fact is that Taylor played a transcendental game."

Vardon tees off at St. Andrews during the 1900 Open Championship, with Old Tom Morris looking on.

Vardon paid no attention to the press and continued to enjoy his respite in Ganton. He played one more match—thirty-six holes versus the best ball of Josiah Livingstone and T. T. Gray at the green of the Edinburgh Burgess Golfing Society at Barnton—and won 3 and 2.

People revered the title of Champion Golfer far more in those days than today, and there was some speculation whether, since he was now the former champion, he would return to America. "Although Harry Vardon has lost the Open Championship of Great Britain, he will return to America and fulfill the dates for exhibition games that have been arranged," reported the *New York Times.* He sailed aboard the *St. Louis* and arrived back in New York on June 27 to news stories that began, "Harry Vardon, former open golf champion of Great Britain, returned to this country yesterday ..."

Vardon was greeted by Charles Cox and Tom Bendelow on the docks in New York, and the three adjourned to the Broadway Central Hotel to review the schedule and make plans for the second half of the tour. He reflected on his Open title defense to a reporter from the *Times:* "Taylor played a jolly good game and deserved to win. I do not know whether practice for some weeks before the game would have altered the results. I was not on to my game. My approaching and putting were not up to my usual standard. Of course there was

A punchbowl green at Shinnecock.

Playing the home hole at Shinnecock.

a difference between the turf here and over there, as well as a difference of atmospheric conditions."

On July 2, Vardon headed to Shinnecock Hills, starting more than five months of matches scheduled around the country. He played a practice round before a large crowd, making a score of 74 that included an inward-half 34. His head-to-head with resident professional Tom Hutchinson was scheduled for the following morning.

"There were at least a thousand persons on the Shinnecock Hills Golf Club links today to see the Vardon-Hutchinson match," reported

The first tee at Shinnecock.

the *Times*, "and they were well repaid for their visit, as it was a fine exhibition of golf. Vardon on his first round equaled the record for the course—70 strokes—made by Hutchinson in practice, and outplayed his man at every point."

If pundits thought Vardon's skills had eroded simply because he was no longer the Open champion, the 12-and-11 defeat of Hutchinson should have changed that perception. Playing out the match, even though the outcome was determined by the seventh hole of the afternoon round, resulted in medal scores of 70 and 71 for the Englishman.

Bringing the Game West

Two days later, Vardon embarked on his first foray to the Midwest, leaving the comfortable confines of Broadway and the New York he had grown fond of. First stop was Cincinnati, where Vardon and Cox checked into the Hotel Honing, "fatigued after the long railway journey" according to the local paper. After some rest, the two were spotted visiting the Cincinnati Zoo in the evening.

Golf had been played on the estate of the Honorable Judge Nicholas Longworth since 1894—one of the earliest outposts in the heartland. When significant interest had been demonstrated by the locals, Longworth laid out nine holes in 1895 and hired Robert White as professional. White was a transplanted Scot who would later become the first president of the PGA of America, and one of the country's foremost pros for decades.

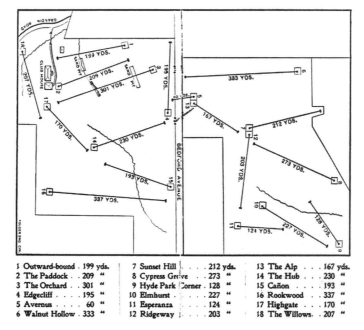

1 Outward-bound	. 199 yds.	7 Sunset Hill	. . . . 212 yds.	13 The Alp	. . . 167 yds.
2 The Paddock	. . 209 "	8 Cypress Grove	. . 273 "	14 The Hub	. . 230 "
3 The Orchard	. . 301 "	9 Hyde Park Corner	. 128 "	15 Cañon	. . 193 "
4 Edgecliff	. . . . 195 "	10 Elmhurst	. . . . 227 "	16 Rookwood	. . 337 "
5 Avernus	. . . . 60 "	11 Esperanza	. . . . 124 "	17 Highgate	. . 170 "
6 Walnut Hollow	. 333 "	12 Ridgeway	. . . . 203 "	18 The Willows	. 207 "

Cincinnati was one of the first eighteen-hole courses in the Midwest.

Date				190
Opponent				

Hole	NAME	Distance Yards	STROKES		Holes
			Self	Opp't	Won by
1	Outward-bound	199			
2	The Paddock	209			
3	The Orchard	301			
4	Edgecliff	195			
5	Avernus	60			
6	Walnut Hollow	333			
7	Sunset Hill	212			
8	Cypress Grove	273			
9	Hyde Park Corner	128			
	Total Yards.	1910			
	Total for 9 Holes out.				
	Total.				
	Handicap.				
	Net.				

Signature

Attest

Date				190
Opponent				

Hole	NAME	Distance Yards	STROKES		Holes
			Self	Opp't	Won by
	Total for 9 Holes out.	1910			
10	Elmhurst	227			
11	Esperanza	124			
12	Ridgeway	203			
13	The Alp	167			
14	The Hub	230			
15	Cañon	193			
16	Rookwood	337			
17	Highgate	170			
18	The Willows	207			
	Total Yards.	3768			
	Total for 9 Holes in.				
	Add First 9 Holes.				
	Total.				
	Handicap.				
	Net.				

Signature

Attest

The yardage for eighteen holes is about the length of a
championship nine-hole loop today.

Robert White

Many of the golf professionals Vardon played against in 1900 were at the middle or end of their careers; Robert White was just starting a lengthy tenure as one of America's most accomplished and respected professionals. White taught school in St. Andrews before emigrating in 1896; Cincinnati was one of many postings in the United States for the man who, in 1916, founded and served as first president of the Professional Golfers Association of America.

As could all his Scottish contemporaries, White could play and teach the game with skill, design and manufacture golf clubs that improved the talent of amateurs, and lay out golf courses that entertained and tested players. But unlike many, White also had a business sense that was respected by club officials; organizational talents that found him heading a Chicago group of professionals who united long before the national group; and greenkeeping skills based on scientific study.

Robert White started a long and distinguished career in American golf at Cincinnati.

Unable to properly drain the clay farmland at Ravisloe, a Chicago-area course he designed and administered, White attended winter agriculture classes at the University of Wisconsin over the course of eleven years. The knowledge he gained and the new inventory of materials applicable to course maintenance that he was able to obtain in Chicago led to an understanding and advancement of golf course agronomy that was sorely needed in an era of little technical information. Such knowledge was part of White's makeup as the consummate golf professional of the era.

In 1899, White added nine holes to the original track, but the course was still a short one, measuring only 3,768 yards. Vardon went around in 66 and 65 during two Friday practice rounds, preparing for a pair of eighteen-hole matches on Saturday, July 7. "Harry Vardon, the English ex-champion, was the great attraction at the Cincinnati Golf Club grounds today," announced the *Chicago Tribune,*

Chicago's Midlothian Country Club was one of the most elegant and cultured golfing centers in the country at the turn of the century.

"about 1,000 devotees of the game and leading society people being present."

In the morning, Vardon played White and won by 3 over eighteen holes. The afternoon he played the best ball of Longworth and Spotwood D. Bowers with the same result. In both games he carded 70. That night, he left for the Windy City.

Vardon's visit to Chicago had been highly anticipated. Tired of playing the proverbial second fiddle to New York golfers, this "Western" enclave felt it could challenge Vardon and was ready to stake its claim on the former champion. Challenges had been issued, and a certain amount of 1900-style trash talking from the Chicago pros appeared in print, probably created from next to nothing by the media. Vardon was booked for three matches at Midlothian with subsequent games at Chicago Golf Club and Glen View. "Vardon, looking brown and hearty, seems in the best of health and spirits," reported the *Tribune*. "He is more than pleased with his reception by the golfers of America and with the preparations made for him during his stay in Chicago." Vardon and Cox checked into the Hotel Normandie, which would serve as their home for two weeks. Vardon had enjoyed the company of Willie Smith in Florida, and the host pro and a few chums called upon his arrival. Chicago city life pleased him almost as much as New York; he attended the theater and toured the landmarks in his off time.

Putting at Midlothian.

A large, square sand field at Midlothian.

Vardon also expressed his pleasure in the outcome of the 1900 U.S. Amateur, just completed at Garden City in New York. "He picked Travis to win after meeting both the new champion and Findlay Douglas in ball matches, believing Travis played the strongest as well as the steadiest game," noted the *Tribune*.

An article in the July 1899 issue of *Outing* magazine called Midlothian "a giant in its infancy [that] has deservedly won the admiration and respect of the Chicago golf public." The course was designed by H. J. Tweedie, a transplant from Royal Liverpool in England, a friend of Charles Blair Macdonald, and a member at Chicago Golf Club. Tweedie and his brother L.P. managed the Spalding Brothers sporting goods store in Chicago. Tweedie also served as referee at the Midlothian matches.

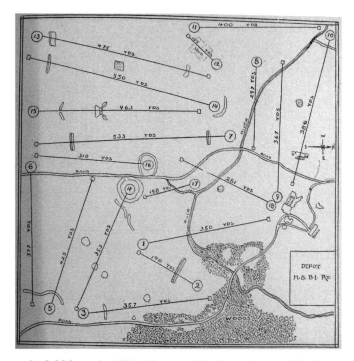

At 6,330 yards, Midlothian was the longest course Vardon
played during his year in America.

At 6,330 yards, Midlothian was the longest course Vardon had
played, and multiple hazards confounded players at nearly every hole.
Harper's Golf Guide added: "The soil is black prairie loam, the turf
firm, close-knit clover and blue grass. Greens large, even and fast."

Vardon took his customary day of practice rounds on July 9, joined
by C. H. Tobey of the Edgewater Club and W. E. Grieve, a Midlothian
pro serving under Willie Smith and David Bell. "He made the course
in 83, three strokes less than the rather liberal bogey figures set by
the club," reported the *Chicago Tribune*. "He did nothing phenomenal,
but all his play was of such an easy, graceful style that he did not
appear to be doing anything out of the way."

Smith, Bell, and Harry Turpie, the Edgewater pro, also played
eighteen with excellent results: Turpie, 82; Bell, 83; Smith, 81. "Should
Turpie and Bell be in as good [as] form today when they meet Vardon,
he will have to be at his best to win," opined the *Tribune*.

He wasn't and they were. Vardon won just three holes in the
thirty-six-hole match before it was decided, and two more as they

played out for medal scores. He fell 6 and 5 to the best ball of the two professionals. "It was generally thought that Vardon would have to do phenomenal work in order to break even with the two local men, but it is nothing out of the ordinary for him to do things which appear wonderful to the ordinary player," noted the *Tribune*.

Although Vardon didn't play his best game, his opponents ham-and-egged it perfectly. Bell could almost keep up with Vardon off the tee, and Turpie had a magnificent short game. At the tenth hole of the morning round Turpie began holing putts that "caused Vardon to inquire if he always putted that way. At six successive holes he found the cup unerringly at dis-

David Bell was one of two pros at Midlothian; he was a long driver and a talented competitor.

tances from eight to twenty feet, his ball seeming to possess some strange affinity for the iron receptacles." Turpie's run left the locals 4 up after the first eighteen, and Vardon never got much closer.

While the morning had been cloudy with rain threatening, the afternoon improved, and many more spectators arrived. They were treated to excellent golf by all three players. But Vardon was not putting well, missing putts to halve holes. He was 5 down after twenty-seven and couldn't muster a charge on the final holes, losing on the thirteenth green. Playing either man separately Vardon would have won, as his twin 82s were the low scores. But outplaying their best ball was beyond his talents that day.

The following day a foursomes or alternate-shot match was contested. Vardon was paired with another "former," Fred Herd, the 1898 U.S. Open champion, playing out of Chicago's Washington Park Club. The host pros—Bell and Smith—were their worthy adversaries, and a steady north wind in the morning gave way to bright sunshine and warmth in the afternoon. No one was really sharp, with Herd the farthest astray. "The play cannot be classed as brilliant," offered the *Tribune,* the first time such frank words had been printed about the tour. "If the quartet had been accused of unprofessional putting the chances are the gallery would have convicted them. Through the whole of the play there were less than five putts that excited any but adverse comment. As a spectator remarked: 'Their putting is almost human.'" Vardon and Herd fell 3 and 2.

After two straight losses Vardon still had one more match at Midlothian—a one-on-one with reigning Open champion Will Smith. The Chicago papers were proud of their pros and predicting a clean sweep, but only Bernard Nicholls had beaten Vardon solo. Vardon played flawlessly save for one bad drive into a ditch. He was 3 up at lunch and cruised to a 4-and-2 win.

"The Midlothian Country Club is entitled to much credit for its generosity in affording the public a chance to see the Englishman free of charge and for the excellent way in which the exhibitions were managed," enthused the *Tribune.* "The transportation of a large crowd in busses a distance of two miles is not a small undertaking, yet all of the visitors were got away without the slightest kind of accident."

If losing two of three matches at Midlothian wasn't enough of a shock, the rest of Vardon's stay in the Chicago area went no better. The day after his match with Smith he was tuning up for a game at Lake Geneva, north of the city. The Lake Geneva Country Club was established on the south shore of the lake in 1897. Robert Foulis designed nine holes for the first summer, and the layout was expanded the following year to a 5,658-yard eighteen-hole course. Lake Geneva was a summer retreat for the wealthy Chicagoans, with many magnificent cottages built on the shoreline of the crystal-clear waters.

On July 13, Vardon played two practice matches. In the morning he played nine holes against the best ball of J. H. Moore, Elmer Williams, and club founder George Walker. Vardon lowered the nine-hole record from 38 to 36 on his first look at the property. But in the afternoon Williams was joined by Nathaniel Moore—a sixteen-year-old rising star of the host club, and Glen View amateur William Holabird Jr. Vardon amazed the crowd with drives of 240 yards, but "his putting at times was indifferent," according to the *Tribune,* and he lost 2 down, with the youngster taking two holes outright.

The following day a large gallery assembled, "including all of Lake Geneva's summer residents and guests," to see if the Midwest could continue its dominance of the great Vardon. Club champion Walter Egan was joined by A.E. Tollifson, the club's professional, and the

James Foulis Jr.

James Foulis Sr. was the shop foreman for Old Tom Morris over the span of thirty-five years, raising each of his five sons around the game at St. Andrews. Together with Robert and David, James Jr. built courses for Old Tom before being enticed to move to Chicago in 1895, where he became the golf professional and close friend of Charles Blair Macdonald. Robert followed James to the Midwest in 1896, and the two collaborated on the design of several courses;

James and David Foulis had an active club and ball business based in Chicago.

David formed J & D Foulis Company with James, and successfully manufactured and marketed golf clubs. Eventually James brought the entire family to America, where each of them flourished in their own ways.

Barrel-chested, strong, and only five feet, five inches tall, James was the most accomplished player in the family and proved it by winning the second U.S. Open. Foulis and Macdonald made the long train ride from Chicago to Shinnecock Hills together in 1896, each to compete in the national championship on the 4,432-yard layout. Foulis closed the tournament with a 74, a score that would not be bettered for seven years. It was good enough for a three-stroke triumph over defending champion Horace Rawlins.

James Foulis Jr. (*right*), winner of the 1896 U.S Open, with brothers David (*left*) and Robert (*center*), three of five golfing brothers from St. Andrews.

Members arrive in style at the Lake Geneva clubhouse.

game was on right from the start, with his opponents buoyed by the success of their compatriots.

Vardon fired a 38 on the first nine holes and stood 1 up. But the locals rallied. "Tollifson started nervously and made some poor drives, but soon recovered and did fine work. He won the seventeenth, holing out in a magnificent putt from the edge of the green. Egan made some fine plays and saved the game several times," reported the *Tribune*. After eighteen, Vardon was 1 down. "Vardon's plays in the afternoon were uniformly better, making each half in 36 and smashing all previous records." But it was not enough as Vardon succumbed to yet another defeat, losing 1 down. Once again it was his putting that abandoned him. "Vardon's drives were nearly all magnificent; his putts were often weak."

A match at Kenosha Golf Club had not been part of the original schedule, but Vardon agreed to appear on July 18. The day prior, with his manager Charles Cox as partner, he lost a practice match to club president George A. Yule and C. H. Tobey of the Edgewater Club, for which the *Tribune* offered this odd excuse: "The ex-champion was at a disadvantage on account of the smallness of the links."

On the following morning Vardon met William Still, the club's professional, and Dr. G. H. Ripley; in the afternoon the thirty-six-hole contest was completed against Chester C. Allen and Yule. "The champion golf team of Kenosha Country Club lowered the colors of champion Vardon this afternoon, defeating the Englishman by a score of 4 up and 3 to play," reported the *Atlanta Constitution*. Counting his practice matches Vardon had now lost six of his last seven contests, and pundits were filling the newspapers with dire predictions for the remainder of his tour. What wasn't reported was he had contracted influenza, compromising his strength and endurance; the illness afflicted him for nearly two weeks.

In 1900 it could easily be argued that Chicago Golf Club was the best golf course in America; surely founder Charles Blair Macdonald thought so. Macdonald had been introduced to golf by Old Tom Morris while a student at St. Andrews University in the early 1870s, and he had waited patiently for America to embrace the game. He founded Chicago Golf in 1892 and moved the course to its current site in 1895, where he laid out the first eighteen-hole course in the United States and continued to improve the property for decades after moving his residence there from New York's Long Island in 1900.

Macdonald's personality was as well known then as his legend is today. He thought a great deal of his own skills, dominated discussions and debates like few others in the golf world, and seldom let reason get in the way of his program. Why, then, he chose not to play Vardon during the ten months he was available in this country is a mystery. He was practically the only player of note in American golf—amateur or professional—who failed to step forward for a match with the English champion.

Vardon appeared at Chicago Golf Club on July 23 and 24. The first morning was wet with showers, "sufficient to slightly dampen the course, the weather clearing shortly after noon, leaving the putting greens in the most favorable condition," according to the *Tribune*. The Club opened its gates to the public, and "many outsiders were present from neighboring towns and clubs to witness the play." Vardon, contrary to expectations, showed no trace of his recent illness and made a game fight against defeat. It was not enough.

Vardon had his hands full versus the best ball of host pro James Foulis and Fred Herd of Washington Park. Shots that strayed off the fairways were hard to extricate from the long grass and usually resulted in a lost hole. Vardon and Herd produced the best long balls, "while Foulis seemed to excel himself in accurate approaching and putting." After the morning round Vardon was 3 down.

Vardon lost another hole by the halfway point of the afternoon circuit but regained it on eleven when "Herd drove into a bunker on his approach and Foulis overdrove the green." But Foulis redeemed himself on the following hole, and shortly after the match was dormie. Vardon fell 6 and 4, and nearly two weeks had passed since he last claimed victory.

That streak changed the following day when Vardon and U.S. Open champion Will Smith renewed their rivalry. It had been more than five months since their first meeting in Florida, when Vardon beat Smith 2 and 1. They had squared off one-on-one again at Midlothian, and Vardon had doubled his margin of victory. But many wondered if Vardon's skid would continue and the third time might be the charm for Smith. Not so, as Vardon came away with another 2-and-1 win. The champion got much more from his visit to Chicago Golf—an appreciation and primer on the course that would host the U.S. Open in October—a tournament that Vardon was very much looking forward to.

One more game remained in Chicago: thirty-six holes against Scot Laurie Auchterlonie at Glen View Golf and Polo Club, where the Scot from St. Andrews was golf professional.

A July 1899 article in *Outing* considered Glen View, located six miles west of Evanston, Illinois, one of the finest courses in the country. "Here a club has been established which has won one of the first places in the galaxy of Chicago organizations. A forest innocent of axe had to be cut out or tunneled through to lay out part of the course, and leveling, sodding, and all kinds of landscape work had to be done; but the results of this outlay of money and labor has been one of the most picturesque courses in the country. The clubhouse is on a knoll in the center of the grounds. Back of the house is a reservoir of clear water, one of the hazards of the course. Sloping greens abound, and altogether the course is a beautiful one, a pleasure to play upon."

The greens at Glen View were in fine condition for Vardon's visit.

Laurie Auchterlonie

Yet another Chicago-area golf pro-fessional raised at St. Andrews, Laurie left his clubmaking brother Willie in St. Andrews when he came to America in 1899 for a position at Glen View. Laurie had remained an amateur in Scotland, even though his brother captured the Open Championship as a pro-fessional in 1893. Once in Amer-ica, Laurie accepted golf as his profession and opened shop in the Windy City, selling clubs designed and manufactured by his brothers who remained back home.

Laurie distinguished himself by placing in the top five at the U.S. Open in five of the first seven

Laurie Auchterlonie was a top competitor in the U.S. Open for a decade, winning the championship in 1902.

years he competed, including a 1902 win at Garden City. There he became the first winner to play the rubber-core ball, defeating club member Walter Travis even though Auchterlonie was seeing the course for the first time. He also became the first player to break 80 in all four rounds, posting 78, 78, 74, and 77 for a six-shot victory.

Early on, Auchterlonie joined the southern exodus of northern pros that followed the warm weather to Florida for the winter. Auchterlonie was installed at the Belleair Country Club in Clearwater, where he joined John Duncan Dunn and other Scottish pros who played exhibitions and competi-tions while the northern clubs were snowed in.

Vardon began with a twenty-seven-hole practice match on July 23 against Phelps B. Hoyt, secretary of the Western Golf Association, and two different partners. In the morning Phelps paired with Frank T. Frazier Jr., who did all the heavy lifting against Vardon, winning one hole and tying Vardon on five others. The pair lost 1 up. In the afternoon Phelps combined with William Holabird Jr., a sixteen-year-old who was the two-time club champion. Phelps's game was suspect from the start, and Holabird understandably suffered from a case of nerves against the world champion. Too, Vardon had finally fully

A water hazard at Glen View.

recovered from his illness and was ready to resume his outstanding form. "From the work of Vardon in the afternoon it would seem that all courses look alike to him," marveled the *Tribune*. "After the first few holes he gave a phenomenal exhibition and played as though he knew the course by heart. Not only was there the machinelike play, but on several occasions he fairly astonished the gallery with little bits of pyrotechnical golf." (Was this reference to what he was smoking or were sparks flying off his clubface?)

The next day brought a quagmire. "The match was played under discouraging conditions, rain falling heavily both in the morning and afternoon, making the greens and course soggy," reported the *Tribune*. "Under the circumstances the two professionals played remarkable golf, and the spectators who braved the weather were well rewarded." Glen View had closed the match to the public; only members were allowed on the property.

Vardon dominated the morning encounter, but Auchterlonie did not give in. When he won the second through fifth holes he brought the match back to level ground. "When he drew even with the man from Ganton the Glen View members did not fail to give him a generous round of applause. After getting even he had the nerve to

These pros gathered at Belmont Golf Club in anticipation of Vardon's participation in an invitational tournament, but Vardon had other plans.

get the Britisher one down, but on the home journey Auchterlonie made several mistakes." Those cost the challenger the game, for even though they matched 77s on the second round, Vardon won 3 and 2 to end his largely unsuccessful Chicago foray.

Or not quite. Belmont Golf Club—actually the site of the first nine-hole Chicago Golf Club, designed by Charles Blair Macdonald, but then renamed when the club moved to Wheaton—had arranged a tournament that it was expecting Vardon to play in. In an article titled "Vardon Afraid to Come?" the *Tribune* claimed the local pros were perturbed. "Some of them hint he is a little afraid he may not carry off first honors when opposed to a field containing many of the best professional champions of the country."

The article went on to say that the tournament would "undoubtedly be the biggest of its kind ever held in the West," and when Vardon had made a verbal agreement to play Belmont had sent invitations to clubs around the country. Furthermore, the club claimed that the tournament had originally been set for July 14 but to accommodate Vardon had been moved to July 28. Vardon and Cox had reserved rooms at the club and engaged James Foulis to play a practice round. "Should he fail to play the officials feel they have not been accorded sportsmanlike treatment," the article claimed.

Clubhouse at the Grosse Pointe links of the Country Club of Detroit.

By the evening edition, Charles Cox offered a reply. "Mr. Vardon had no agreement to play in the Belmont club tournament on Saturday. I was asked several times to enter Mr. Vardon and eventually did so. It has since become impossible for Mr. Vardon to play there because of other and more pressing business engagements so I withdrew the entry several days ago. There was no agreement at all—I just entered him and withdrew him. There is no ill feeling nor broken promises in the case whatsoever." That was subject to debate.

Vardon left Chicago with a bad taste in his mouth, but a vow to change the mood in October at the Open. The best thing he acquired in the Windy City was some experience on the links of the Chicago Golf Club, and that was as good as money in the bank.

Meanwhile it was on to the more "pressing business engagements"—i.e., the ones that paid $250 per appearance—in other cities. The Country Club of Detroit at Grosse Pointe had been established in 1898, and *Harper's Official Golf Guide* called it a "well-turfed course, with rather stiff hazards and fine putting greens." The eighteen holes measured a scant 4,825 yards, and W. H. "Bert" Way was golf professional and greenkeeper. Way was a product of Royal North Devon Golf Club in England, had caddied for J. H. Taylor in the mid-1880s, and came to America in 1896. He designed the Detroit layout and later in 1898 moved to Cleveland, where he spent the rest of his career. He was also instrumental in developing the rubber-core golf ball with his friend Coburn Haskell.

"A crowd of 300 members of the Country Club and elite of Detroit society watched Harry Vardon, the former champion golf player of England, trim W. H. Way of Detroit. Vardon played a faultless game and defeated Way in all points of the game. The Englishman's stroke

The eighteenth green at Grosse Pointe.

Crowds gather to see Vardon in Detroit.

was clean, precise, and effective," concluded the *New York Times.* Vardon fired a pair of 68s on the layout, equaling Way's course record and beating the host 8 and 7. The *Chicago Tribune,* with its typical convoluted golf copy, added: "Vardon's methods were a revelation to

The nine-hole Cleveland Golf Club in Glenville, Ohio.

Joe Mitchell, the greenkeeper who helped Coburn Haskell develop the rubber-core ball, faced off against Vardon in Cleveland.

the golfists of this city, and a wrecking in local records may be expected as a result."

Vardon had one more Midwestern city to visit before the tour headed for the mountains and shorelines of the Northeast. At the nine-hole Cleveland Golf Club in Glenville he beat the best ball of resident pro/greenkeeper Joe Mitchell and Sterling Beckwith 4 and 3. In the process he broke yet another course record, negotiating the nine holes in 33 strokes. With that, Vardon was off to New York, first to the city, then to the Adirondack Mountains.

CHAPTER 6

On Mountains and Seashores

The Wilds of the North

Vardon never made excuses for substandard play. A shoulder injury in Florida and a bout with the flu in Chicago went largely unreported, though both affected his golfing abilities and led to losses. Travel and weather also took their toll on the champion, and Vardon looked forward to a weeklong stay in the relaxed and comfortable surroundings of upstate New York's Adirondack Mountains.

Vardon was lured to Blue Mountain Lake by William West Durant, a legendary figure in the development of the recreational offerings of the Northeast's grandest and most remote mountain range. Durant was born in Brooklyn, educated in England and Germany, and came to the Adirondacks to assist his father in managing the Adirondack Railroad Company. In the 1880s, Durant bought land, developed transportation systems, built hotels and resorts, and designed "great camps" for J. P. Morgan, Alfred Vanderbilt, Seward Webb, and other financial kingpins.

In 1899, Durant spent nearly $70,000 to construct Eagle's Nest Country Club, with a 3,030-yard, nine-hole course designed by Willie Dunn Jr. on the shores of Eagle Lake. Durant wanted nothing less than the greatest golfer in the world to christen his golf course, so he paid Vardon "$500 for the week and a bottle of Scotch whiskey every night," according to J. Peter Martin's 1987 book on *Adirondack Golf Courses.* Vardon took up residence on August 1 and planned several exhibitions for the week.

Apparently Durant could not lure any other top professionals to the mountains to oppose the champion; the matches with the best amateurs were routs that set new records for Vardon. He started with a best-ball practice match, partnered with George Armstrong of Fox Hills Golf Club, versus Harry Roy Sweney of Albany Country Club and Mortimer Singer. "Vardon's driving was marvelous," gushed the *Boston Globe,* "repeatedly over the 250-yard mark, while his approach shots were equally wonderful. His opponents had no chance whatever against him."

After weeks in the Midwest, Vardon was comforted by the site of Eagle's Nest Country Club on Blue Mountain Lake in New York's Adirondack Mountains.

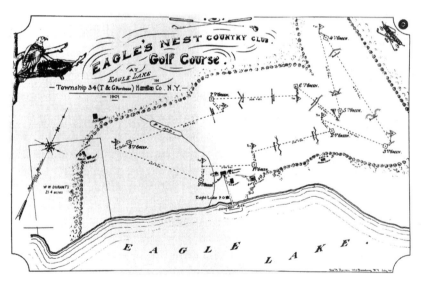

Eagle's Nest lakeside layout was designed by Willie Dunn Jr.

The following day Vardon took on Armstrong and Singer, and the results reflected his natural talent, recovered health, and peaceful comfort in the mountain environment. Over the course of thirty-six holes the amateurs managed to win two holes with their best ball.

GOLF.

ADMISSION CARDS TO EAGLE'S NEST COUN-
TRY CLUB AND GOLF COURSE FOR THE

HARRY VARDON EXHIBITION,
Aug. 1st to Aug. 7th, 1900,

CAN BE OBTAINED AT RAQUETTE LAKE RAILWAY
STATION, RAQUETTE LAKE, N. Y., ON STEAMBOATS
AT RAQUETTE LAKE AND BLUE MT. LAKE AND AT
PRINCIPAL HOTELS IN VICINITY.

Single Day, $1.00   Entire Week, $3.00

Vardon's stay at Eagle's Nest was the longest of the tour.

A challenging hazard at Eagle's Nest.

Vardon shot 75 in the morning round and was 12 up after eighteen holes. Technically he closed the match on the fourth green of the afternoon round with a tally of 15 and 14, but the remaining holes were contested for the benefit of the spectators, and Vardon ended 22 up, even though over the last nine holes "Vardon conceded half a stroke, and as a further handicap played the last hole with his putter." He still managed to post a bogey 5 to his competitors' 6 on the thirty-sixth hole, using just the flat stick.

A little Scotch, a few nights rest, some outdoor diversions, and Vardon was ready for another match on August 5 against Stuart Gillispie of Fairfield County Golf Club and Sweney of Albany. "Lovers of golf were treated to one of the best exhibitions yet given [by Vardon] in this country," claimed the *New York Times*. "His card over 36 holes only showed two sixes, which is all the more remarkable when it is considered that the course is fully 3,000 yards, and the two sixes represented his play on the same hole twice—namely, the fourth, which is 500 yards long." Vardon beat his own course record—twice, scoring 74 in the morning and 71 in the afternoon. He was 19 up on his opponent's best ball when all the holes were played.

One incident in the match was reported by magazines and newspapers around the world. "His ball on the carry from the tee at the fourth hole struck a rock and bounded partly off the course, lodging on the side of a rotten stump about two feet from the ground," reported *Golf* magazine. "Vardon took his driver, and with half a swing around his shoulder drove the ball 230 yards, stuck his club in the caddie bag, and walked on as though he had played an ordinary stroke." It was as if to say, "This, America, is how a world champion approaches the game."

His final match on August 7 featured Oscar Bunn, the professional at the Lake Placid Club, and George Stevens, one of the club's best amateurs. "The couple were never in it for a single instance, and seemed to suffer from stage fright," surmised the *Times*. The score was another 12-up win for Vardon; the difference being that this game was only eighteen holes. The champion made 74; the best ball of his opponents a dismal 95. Whatever malaise had befallen Vardon in the Midwest was gone; after a week in the mountains he was refreshed, recharged, and ready for battle. He ended his stay by visiting Lake Placid, calling it "extremely enjoyable," but no golf match was reported.

From the mountains, Vardon was off to the seashore, arriving at the Portland Golf Club in Falmouth, Maine, on August 10. Golf had been played around Portland since 1895, with a formal course and organization incorporated by April of 1898. *Golf* called the soil similar to the seaside golf links of Scotland: "The whole field may be called an undulating hill of sand, formed in an earlier geological period, with a light loam on the surface. There is no clay to bake hard under the summer sun. The land was originally farming land, in a high state of cultivation. The ground is therefore smooth, free from stones and trees, and supports a light, springy turf. The club has reason to be proud of the length of its course. The playing distance, 3,094 yards, is nearly the same as on the best Scottish and English links, and much better than the average American."

For the third time Vardon squared off against Alex Findlay; they would go on to play another dozen times together. The weather was

The clubhouse at the Portland Golf Club in Maine.

Typical embanked bunkers snake across two fairways at Portland.

a challenge. "The day was intensely hot and the high wind, which was like a blast from a furnace, not only seemed to increase the heat but effectually prevented the carrying of umbrellas," reported the *Portland Telegram*. A "large and fashionable audience" assembled, with patrons coming from many of the golf clubs in southern Maine on specially scheduled trains. One estimate put the crowd at two thousand.

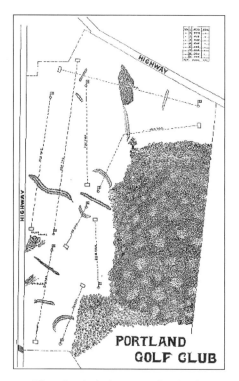

The nine-hole layout at Portland.

Findlay played brilliantly in the morning round, matching Vardon stroke for stroke. "At the end of the first half Findlay was one up," crowed the *Telegram.* "He has played here before and had many personal friends who were at fever pitch of excitement. Vardon was of course a stranger to the links, never having been so far East before." But then disaster struck in the afternoon. "Findlay broke his cleek early in the game and his pet brassey mysteriously disappeared which was something of a handicap." The reporter's observation was a gross understatement, as Findlay then had no long-distance clubs to use from the fairway. Vardon brought the match to square on the third hole and "After that, however, the Boston player was not able to take a hole, so steadily did Vardon play." The result was a 6-and-4 win.

Vardon's play on the third hole created a buzz that echoed for years in Portland. "His most remarkable shot of the day was a 300-yard drive on the third hole—The Bend—in the second round," noted Portland's club history book. "A 50-foot oak tree about 190 yards from the tee marked the corner of the sharp dogleg. Vardon tried to drive over the tree—which had never been done before—and succeeded. He went 100 yards past the tree." Vardon, in fact, cleared the tree on the 420-yard hole three of the four times he played it, with the longest strike concluding just 120 yards from the green. Taking the sharp bend into consideration, his drive probably did not travel 300 yards, but the lore surrounding his driving skills increased the distance of the tee ball as the years passed. Vardon's driving skills were legendary, especially since most amateurs averaged only about 140 yards off the tee in 1900. "His long, straight driving was something that probably no living man can equal," stated the Portland paper. "He seemed to throw every ounce of energy possessed into his shots."

Vardon drives at the Poland Spring Inn while Fenn and Findlay (both in white pants) and a large crowd look on.

Though Vardon was held in public awe at nearly every stop on his journey, his private reception at the clubs varied. This was still the era where professionals, no matter how talented, were working-class, whereas private golf clubs were the retreats of the social elite. At the resorts and public courses Vardon was not only allowed to demonstrate his skill but also made to feel comfortable in the facilities.

A short way from Portland was the Poland Spring House, one of the first resort courses in America. Poland Spring was the home of Arthur Fenn, a Waterbury, Connecticut, native who had achieved considerable notoriety as an amateur, winning the Lenox Cup three times before the turn of the century. Staged at the Lenox Country Club in the Berkshires of Massachusetts, the Cup was one of early American golf's greatest prizes, second only to the U.S. Amateur trophy. Fenn turned professional after his run and began a twenty-five-year tenure as the pro at Poland Spring.

Vardon and Findlay arrived on August 12, and Fenn showed them a relaxing time in the hills of western Maine. First they enjoyed a sail on Range Pond, then a ten-mile coach ride over the Poland hills. A lavish dinner with many toasts and tributes followed, concluding in the smoking room with a glass of Scotch. Having met six months earlier in Florida, the three were now comfortable friends.

Overlooking the Poland Spring links from the top floor of the grand hotel.

Square greens were a feature of Poland Spring.

In the morning, Vardon and Fenn squared off in a thirty-six-hole match. "The day opened with rain and the start was delayed half an hour, when the sky cleared and the day was perfect for good golf," reported *The Hill-Top,* Poland's own weekly newspaper. "A large gallery of hotel guests followed the players throughout the match, and applauded each good stroke." Fenn put up a good fight but lost not

Vardon launches an opening drive at the Mount Pleasant House while
Alex Findlay waits his turn at the back of the tee.

only the match, 7 and 6, but also the course record, as Vardon set
the nine-hole record at 36 and the eighteen-hole mark with 72.

The next day there was a best-ball contest. Fenn and Findlay
played more competitive golf together than any other pair in America,
both as partners and adversaries, touring the Northeast opening new
clubs, setting course records, and spreading the game in any way
they could. The twosome had their "A" game this day and matched
Vardon for the first four holes, then took three in a row, opening a
lead that Vardon could not erase the remainder of the morning round.
Vardon found no better fortune in the afternoon, and his demise
by a score of 2 and 1 could be easily explained. "Fenn and Findlay
won through Vardon's misses of short putts, wherein the hole was
rimmed in each instance," reported the *New York Times*. Whenever
Vardon struggled on his yearlong tour it was due to his putting. While
this can be attributed partly to the variable quality and speed of the
greens, putting was already the weak link in the champion's game,
a shortcoming that would be compounded in the years to come.

Promising to return in two weeks, Vardon and Findlay left Fenn
behind and headed to New Hampshire's White Mountains. Since the
middle of the nineteenth century, magnificent wood-frame hotels had
provided summer respite for wealthy families escaping the summer

Gilbert Nicholls could not find his brother Bernard's magic in his match with Vardon.

The fourth green at Mt. Pleasant in the shadow of Mount Washington.

atmosphere of Philadelphia, New York, and Boston. Many of the resorts embraced golf early, realizing that the summer residents were members at urban clubs and that the best way to keep them for the summer was to provide entertainment, competitions, and plenty of golf. Most of the locales Vardon had visited thus far in 1900 had one golf course; here he played four within a few miles. "Vardon states that he has never seen a larger number of good links within so short a distance of each other," reported the *White Mountain Echo,* a weekly that wrote volumes about the champion's every move.

Vardon and Findlay arrived on the Maine Central from Poland Spring at 12:40 on August 16, and a large crowd awaited them at the platform. They were greeted by the owners and managers of the Mount Pleasant House, the president of the golf club, numerous dignitaries, and the town band. A luncheon followed and then a foursomes practice match on the nine-hole Mount Pleasant House links. Vardon and Findlay played the host professional, Charlie Thom, and Gilbert Nicholls, who was visiting from Boston. Gilbert was the brother of Bernard Nicholls, who had defeated Vardon at Ormond Beach in Florida. Though it was just a practice match a large crowd gathered to watch Vardon. "With his very first drive, all spectators were filled with admiration for the champion, and this admiration grew as the match continued," claimed *Among the Clouds,* a summer daily published from the top of Mount Washington. "Under the direction of the management the spectators were kept out of the way of the players by means of long ropes." Vardon and Findlay won the eighteen-hole contest 3 up.

The next day started with thunderstorms, and patrons were concerned that the thirty-six-hole affair between Vardon and the best ball of Thom and Findlay would have to be scratched. But after a short delay the game was on and so were Vardon's skills. He posted 68 in the morning, a new record and six better than the best ball of Thom and Findlay, who each shot 80. Vardon's lowest tally of the nine-hole loop was a 32. "Thrice when Thom and Findlay were hugging the hole with their seconds, Vardon was 50 yards away and on each occasion holed out and robbed his hard-plodding opponents out of three holes," reported the *White Mountain Echo.* The champion's approaches were sunk from 55, 48, and 15 yards from the cup.

To everyone's amazement Vardon trimmed yet another stroke from the record score in the afternoon, turning in a 67. "Vardon's score of 135 betters the previous record by twenty strokes, and his driving was the longest ever seen here," concluded the *Echo.* Needless to say it was another victory for Vardon, this time by 5 and 4.

One of Vardon's favorite shots was a trick he practiced and occasionally used in tight circumstances on the golf course. "After the match Mr. Vardon was requested to repeat his Portland and Poland Springs feats of driving a ball tied on a bush straight into the air, which he did, the ball rising at least 150 yards, and coming down in close proximity to the starting point. Not only did he do this once, but six times consecutively at Portland."

The show moved to the Maplewood Golf Club in Bethlehem on Friday with another foursome practice match. This time Vardon was paired with David Findlay—brother of Alex and resident pro at

Charlie Thom

A native of Montrose, Scotland, Thom started as a caddie; in 1894, at age fourteen, he became an apprentice to clubmaker James Winton. He intended to pursue his education with hopes of being a doctor, but finances conspired against him, and shortly after his apprenticeship he came to the United States for a job at the Shelter Island Golf Links on Long Island. For a while Thom split his time between Shelter Island and teaching at the Spalding indoor golf school in New York City, until he was hired at the Mount Pleasant House. After two seasons in New Hampshire, Thom gravitated southward, taking a position at Lenox Golf Club in Massachusetts. Eventually, in 1906, he found a permanent home at Shinnecock Hills in Southampton.

Thom was Shinnecock's only pro from 1906 to 1961, an amazing span of fifty-five years in service to some of America's most famous and wealthy patrons. He treated them all with courtesy and respect, the same behavior he bestowed upon the caddies, suppliers, and maintenance workers. Thom was comfortable breaking in on meetings of J. P. Morgan; telling Andrew Mellon to stop worrying about his investments and keep his eye on the ball; and repairing a hickory golf club for

Charlie Thom played Vardon at the Mount Pleasant House and later served as the golf professional at Shinnecock from 1906 to 1961.

a member's child who had borrowed the parental clubs without permission. Charlie had a soft spot for the kids, often finding them inundating his shop to eat chocolates and practice their putting. Even after he officially retired, Thom remained at Shinnecock to help with events, living in a small cottage near the tee of the fourteenth hole—a hole aptly named Thom's Elbow.

Vardon drives at Mt. Pleasant.

Maplewood—versus Alex and Charles Cox. The result was the same with the former pair prevailing 3 up in twenty-one holes.

Saturday brought favorable weather and a crowd estimated at 400 for "one of the grandest sights ever witnessed at the Maplewood." Vardon played the best ball of the Findlay brothers, marking the first time the siblings had played together since their days as kids in Montrose, Scotland. The brothers drew first blood with a win on the second hole, a harbinger of things to come. But Vardon fought back, and on the ninth "Vardon took his mashie and holed out in two amid great applause from the many spectators," reported the *White Mountain Echo*. That gave the champion a 35, a new course record by three, and a 3-up lead. At the same hole later on, Alex Findlay made a long putt to close out the morning round only 2 down.

In the afternoon Vardon was once again 3 up with just eight holes to play when "the Findlay brothers began work in earnest." They won five of the next six holes, and when Alex halved the seventeenth they had a hard-won 2-and-1 victory.

Sunday was a day of rest, and the Englishman took time to enjoy the fabulous excursions available in the heart of the White Mountains. Trails had been cut to many of the mountaintops, and horse-drawn

The Maplewood casino has long been a White Mountain attraction.

The Waumbek links were split by a railroad station and tracks and
bordered by the elegant cottages of the members.

carriages were common on precipitous pathways transporting visitors
to revealing outlooks and natural phenomena that had thrilled city
dwellers for decades. There was little regard for the danger involved,
but the sure-footedness of the horses allowed better access than
the thin tires of the automobiles that would attempt to follow in the
years to come.

The Profile House course was designed by Arthur Fenn and surrounded by spectacular scenery.

After sightseeing, it was on to Waumbek Golf Club in Jefferson on Monday, and what was widely regarded as the center of northern New England golf. The Waumbek hotel was the first lodging built in town in 1860; it was followed by other hotels wishing to capitalize on the stunning views of the Presidential Range of high peaks to the south and east. Willie Norton designed nine holes in 1895, and Arthur Fenn doubled the layout in 1899—creating the first eighteen-hole course in the state. A full schedule of matches and tournaments attracted the best players in America to this remote mountain outpost; and when the club engaged the services of Horace Rawlins, its prestige was assured.

Monday afternoon brought the traditional foursomes practice match at Waumbek, with Vardon and club amateur J. Whitney Baker opposing Alex Findlay and E. M. Dalley of the home club. The former team won on the nineteenth green.

"Perfect golfing weather favored the enthusiasts Tuesday for the contest between Harry Vardon and the best ball of A. H. Findlay and Horace Rawlins, the Waumbek professional," reported the *Echo*. Vardon was still struggling on the greens. "His playing during the morning was remarkable for its steadiness, though his putting was not quite as good as had been expected."

At the ninth hole, "one of the most beautiful plays ever witnessed on a golf course took place when each man placed the ball on the green within close proximity to the flag, a distance of 210 yards." Vardon failed to convert his putt and fell 4 down after nine holes.

Horace Rawlins

The stunning victory of nineteen-year-old Horace Rawlins in the inaugural U.S. Open was considered a fluke, and even though Rawlins never won the national championship again he proved his mettle with many years of competent golf. The *New York Times* described his game as "well balanced, strong in all its elements, yet brilliant in none. He is a good heady player with a happy faculty of not getting discouraged when in difficulties." Rawlins posted a second place the following year, but after the 1909 tournament, when he finished dead last, 39 strokes off the winning total, Rawlins resigned from competitive golf. Eventually he gave up professional golf entirely and, after the death of his mother in 1914, returned to England to work as a draper.

Horace Rawlins, winner of the first U.S. Open in 1895, played Vardon at Waumbek, where he was the pro in 1900.

As the first U.S. Open champion, the young Rawlins was pursued by a number of clubs who desired his services and the prestige of employing the Open champion. After the season at Newport the English pro spent two years at Sadaquada Golf Club near Utica, New York; helped his brother Harry establish the Hillside Golf Club for the Equinox Hotel in southern Vermont; moved to Waumbek in the White Mountains of New Hampshire; built the Springhaven Club outside of Philadelphia; spent two years at Wykagyl near New York City; and finally settled in at Ekwanok in the Green Mountains.

Although Vardon lowered Findlay's course record by a shot to 76, he concluded the morning round 3 down to the professionals.

In the afternoon, reported the *Echo,* "Oftentimes Vardon found his ball buried in deep grass, ditches and bunkers and everyone wondered how he would be enabled to extricate himself. He not only got clear of such obstacles, but placed the majority of such shots on the green." Despite his recovery expertise, Vardon fell 4 and 3.

A final singles match in the White Mountains was played at the Fenn-designed Profile House links on Thursday, August 23, and Findlay had run out of steam, losing to the champion 11 and 10. Vardon wrote a letter to the Club that it has cherished ever since. "I have yet to see a lovelier place, or one with more natural advantages for golf, than the Profile House Links," claimed Vardon. Anyone who has visited this comely site in the hundred-plus years since would have to agree. Vardon went on to say, "Other clubs might well copy the way the Profile Club does in the matter of grass tees, and piped greens, and with a good wet spring next year it will be a course anybody will be delighted to play on."

As promised, Vardon and Findlay returned to Poland Spring on August 25, after their mountain sojourn. In another best-ball match against Fenn and Findlay, Vardon triumphed 4 and 2. However, the local pair had not lured their friend back to Poland Spring just to be beaten again; they had something else in mind that was revealed that evening.

"As Vardon entered the great hall of the hotel, accompanied by his two opponents of the day, the entire company cheered," noted the *Boston Globe*. "Vardon was presented with a cup by his admirers. B. P. Moulton of Philadelphia made a graceful speech, to which Vardon responded in a few modest words, after which the entire company sang, 'God Save the Queen,' 'America,' and 'The Star Spangled Banner.' The presentation of the cup proved one of the most pleasing events of the whole golfing season at the resort. Mr. Findlay was then called upon and made a bright speech full of witticisms on the peculiarities of the game." Don't you wish you could see a video of that?

Kebo's membership included some of the wealthiest people in America.

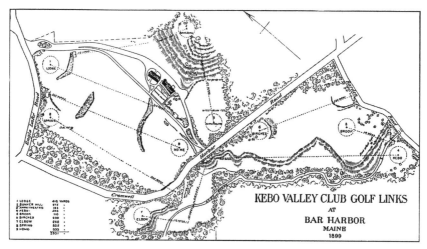

KEBO VALLEY CLUB GOLF LINKS
AT
BAR HARBOR
MAINE
1899

Kebo's challenge came from terrain, water hazards, and cross bunkers.

After his most enjoyable interlude in the mountains and at Poland Spring, Vardon arrived in Bar Harbor, Maine, on August 26. One of the foremost playgrounds of America's wealthiest, Mt. Desert Island is unsurpassed for scenic splendor; there the tallest mountains on the Eastern seaboard are caressed by the wild waters of the North Atlantic. The Kebo Valley Club was established in 1888, and members included George Vanderbilt, Joseph Pulitzer, John Jacob Astor, Seward Webb, Charles Beaman, Edsel Ford, Augustus Hemenway, DeGrasse Fox, James P. Scott, Robert Amory, DeWitt Cuyler, Robert Guggenheim, and John D. Rockefeller. Horse racing was the first love of the patrons, though golfing grounds infiltrated the race track oval early in the 1890s. Herbert Leeds of Boston was the golfing patriarch, and his six-hole course was already in use during the 1894 season. By 1898, Leeds and Waldron Bates extended it to nine holes, measuring 2,810 yards with a bogey of 40. *Harper's Official Golf Guide* noted about the course "a good fair-green constantly being improved, and large, undulating, and true putting greens." Leeds and Vardon had met at the Palmetto Club in South Carolina in March, and it was hoped his reception at Kebo would be warmer than the unpleasant reception he had encountered from the members there.

Vardon, Findlay, and Cox checked into the Newport House and arranged a practice match for the first afternoon. While Findlay went sightseeing, Vardon and Cox were paired against pro/greenkeeper

Golf had been played at the Kebo Valley Club in Maine longer than nearly every other club Vardon visited.

James Douglas and Dr. Cushman of St. Louis in an 18-hole match they won easily. The following day saw the first of two 36-hole contests.

"It was a sizzling hot day for Bar Harbor," noted the *Boston Daily Globe,* "but the heat had no effect upon Vardon, who made a new record of 75 for the 18 holes. He said the greens at Kebo were the finest he had seen in this country and that those in Detroit approached them the closest. Those in England and Scotland, he said, were not appreciably better." Beside Shinnecock Hills, Kebo's course was the most mature layout he had played, having been in use for seven seasons upon his arrival. Vardon played the best ball of Herbert Jaques and Harvard golfer George O. Thacher, cruising to a 6-and-5 win. The following day Thacher sought the help of local golf pro Douglas, but the results were no different: Vardon won 8 and 7.

The Comfort of the South

Traveling from the Adirondacks to Down East Maine in 1900 must have been an eye-opener for Vardon after the urban scenes of America's Midwest. There were far more pine trees than roads, a greater number of cows than people. Northern New England featured breathtaking vistas rather than throat-clogging city smog. But Vardon returned to more populated southern New England on the last day of August for a match at the George Wright–designed Allston Golf Club in Massachusetts. Organized in 1897, Allston's nine-hole course

VARDON BREAKS ALLSTON LINKS RECORD.

In His Match With Alex Findlay He Wins 4 Up 3 to Play, and Does Some Remarkable Driving.

HOW THE GALLERY FOLLOWED VARDON AND FINDLAY.

Headlines from an article in the *Boston Globe* on September 2, 1900.

was a meager 2,063 yards long, and both men easily surpassed the previous course record in the morning. In the afternoon Vardon trimmed another five strokes from the standard, firing a 65 to drop Findlay by 5 and 4.

"Such golf has not been seen in this vicinity since he played the best ball matches at Wollaston early this spring," claimed the *Globe*. "In the forenoon he was not feeling well, yet he played a splendid game, his only noticeable fault being in putting. But it was in the afternoon that the golfing enthusiasts saw the wonderful game he is capable of playing. He used a decidedly low tee, whenever he did tee the ball, and with a lightning-like swing he shot the white sphere away on its journey with splendid direction and for grand distances."

It had been difficult for Cox to arrange a match at the Newport Golf Club in Rhode Island despite the fact the club was one of the finest in America, site of the first U.S. Open and a founding member

The Allston clubhouse.

of the USGA. The same social elite who frequented Kebo Valley circulated at Newport, but the club was reticent to advance the required stipend. It wasn't until August 21 that the *New York Times* announced that "William H. Sands, who has done much toward booming the playing there this season, has guaranteed Mr. Vardon's expenses and salary." Sands was a three-time club champion at St. Andrew's in New York and part of a well-to-do golfing family.

Without the benefit of a practice round, Vardon confronted amateurs R. C. Watson Jr. of Westbrook in Islip, New York, and Charles Hitchcock Jr., a multiple tournament winner in 1900, in an

R. C. Watson Jr. was one of two amateurs who opposed Vardon in a morning match at Newport.

eighteen-hole morning game. "In going out he was 3-up, Watson and Hitchcock having been a little unsteady in such fast company. The play of the amateurs was steadier coming in," noted the *Boston*

Willie Norton

One of the first golf professionals to arrive in America, Willie Norton came from Scotland's Prestwick in November 1894. He was immediately engaged by the Golf Club of Lakewood in New Jersey, a position he held many years, while designing courses and participating in challenge matches elsewhere. Norton was the only man in America who played Vardon and Taylor in 1900, and he also faced Willie Park Jr., squaring off in singles and foursomes against Park at Lakewood in May of 1895.

The following summer, Norton laid out the original nine holes at the Waumbek in Jefferson, New Hampshire, the first nine-hole course in the White Mountains. Norton also added nine to Lakewood and designed an eighteen-hole course for Seabright Golf Club in New Jersey. Norton split his time between Seabright and Lakewood, and then, after five years, Lakewood and the Deal Golf Club. He gave many lessons and taught a large segment of New Jersey's early amateur contingent how to play the game in the Scottish style.

His own game was anchored by his putting and chipping. After playing Vardon at Seabright he partnered with R. B. Wilson to face the best ball of J. H. Taylor at Deal. "In the match with Taylor his work on the green was remarkable, and was largely responsible for the English player's defeat," wrote *Golf* magazine of Taylor's first game in America. "Taylor himself bore the strongest testimony to this when he said, 'If someone would steal Norton's putter, I might have a chance to win.' Norton is one of those professionals who do credit to the game, and he is deservedly popular and respected."

Globe. Still, Vardon triumphed on the eighteen-hole course by 2 up. In the afternoon the pros took center stage, and host James Stronner teamed with Findlay. "The Newport professional knew the course well, which gave him a great advantage over Vardon," and the team converted that to a 4-and-2 victory. Few details of the match ever appeared in the media.

Vardon and Findlay ventured onto Cape Cod before heading to New Jersey. At the time, few could have guessed that the future of the sandy fishhook would be so tied to golf, for in 1900 Cape Cod supported just a few short courses. The 2,907-yard, nine-hole Seapuit Golf Club in Osterville was one of the best; the club had been established in 1893, only to vanish in the 1930s. Vardon and Findlay played an eighteen-hole practice match on September 4, with Vardon winning 79 to 81.

The Seabright Golf Club on the coast of New Jersey was an important early golfing outpost; a course was established in 1895 and expanded to eighteen holes by Willie Norton in 1897. Norton split his time between Seabright and Lakewood, in addition to playing in tournaments and dabbling in course architecture. When Vardon announced his visit to Seabright the speculative debate in the press was whether he could beat the score J. H. Taylor had made on the links three weeks previously. Taylor had been touring the United States since shortly after his victory in the 1900 Open Championship, and everyone in America—except apparently Vardon and Taylor—were comparing their talents and waiting for a golfing showdown.

Though not part of the head-to-head match everyone craved, Vardon's performance at Seabright bested the earlier showing by Taylor. "Record Golf by Vardon" headlined the *New York Times* article, which had the subhead "He Lowers Taylor's Score by Two Strokes for the Seabright Links." A practice four-ball on September 7 pitted Vardon and club amateur Dr. W. Gill Wylie against Norton and Amos T. Dwight, "a Yale student who recently won the amateur championship of the club." Vardon posted 71 on the 5,276-yard layout, eclipsing Taylor's 73 of three weeks previous. In the afternoon, a best-ball foursome was played, with Norton and Dwight teaming up for a 3-and-1 win over Vardon and Wylie.

On the following day Vardon faced Norton and F. W. Menzies, a top amateur player, and a close match resulted. Though Vardon beat each of the men individually, he could not conquer their best ball. The champion lost the thirtieth hole to squander a 1-up advantage, lost again on the thirty-third, and fought all the way home but succumbed to the pair by 1 up.

Less Than a Month to the Open

Since his defeat at St. Andrews in the Open Championship, Vardon had been focused on the U.S. Open, scheduled for October 4 at the Chicago Golf Club. Golf fans took their national championships seriously, and Vardon was growing tired of being referred to as the "former champion" of Britain and wished to annex a new prefix to his name.

He arrived at the Essex County Club in Manchester-by-the-Sea, Massachusetts, on September 11, and under partly sunny skies played two 18-hole practice matches with club professional Joseph Lloyd. Vardon defeated Lloyd in both contests and set a new course record of 73 in the process.

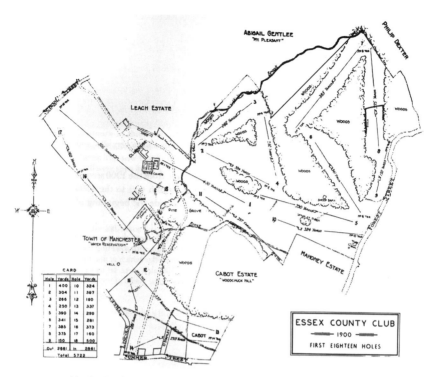

Vardon's visit officially opened the difficult Essex course.

The Essex course was carved from woods over severe terrain.

The next day featured the most challenging weather of the entire trip, over a course that was far from ideal. "It was a day wholly unfavorable to golf," announced the *Boston Globe*. "This gale, a hurricane almost, began in the early morning, and at 10 o'clock, when play began, it was howling along at the rate of 45 miles an hour. The spectators at the first teeing ground experienced no little difficulty in maintaining their stand against it, and hats, caps, etc., were easy victims, being swept all over the course by the unrelenting gusts. Nor was the

Vardon tees his ball on number one at Essex County Club to
inaugurate the new eighteen-hole course.

wind the only thing the players and spectators had to face, as great
clouds of dust, sand, leaves, and little twigs snapped off the trees were
continually hurled in their faces, and the heat was unbearable."

Vardon was playing the best ball of the two Essex professionals, Joseph Lloyd and Jack Dingwall, at the debut of the club's new
eighteen-hole course. Evidence suggests that the new course was
created from the suggestions of Herbert Leeds, Walter Travis, and
John Duncan Dunn, but the site left a great deal to be desired. The
Globe claimed that "a more unpromising spot for a golf course than
this could not well be imagined. Through the very heart of the woods
it ran, up one side and down the other side of steep hills, over high,
rocky cliffs and through a swamp." The article reported that a hundred men had blasted thousands of cubic yards of rock and piled up
a thousand cords of wood to create the 5,722-yard layout. "The new
nine holes have been made over country which at one time looked
hopeless. The work of hewing trees, blasting rocks, and removing
undergrowth has been titanic," reported *Golf* magazine.

In the early years of American golf course architecture, imitating
the courses of Great Britain was paramount to success, and trees
were not considered part of a high-quality layout. The Essex track
wound its way through "narrow lanes" of forest, surely an oddity to
Vardon. "When one realizes that the men had to go through these
'lanes' with a howling gale interfering, and with Vardon only having

Joe Lloyd

Probably the most talented golfer Vardon faced during his 1900 tour, Lloyd began as a caddie at Hoylake in Cheshire, England, later becoming an assistant there to pro Jack Morris, a nephew of Old Tom. Known as "The General," Lloyd was appointed golf professional at the Golf Club of Pau in France in the late 1880s, a job he continued to hold for many years. Even after Lloyd came to Massachusetts's Essex County Club in 1895, he split his time between the two outposts—serving at Essex in the summer and returning to Pau each winter.

Lloyd won the 1897 U.S. Open at Chicago Golf Club in dramatic fashion. The *Chicago Tribune* described his play on the final hole of the championship: "It is 400 yards from teeing ground to hole. Lloyd drove 270 yards, following with a superb brassie shot which laid the ball on the green ten feet from the hole. A less experienced and steady golfer would probably have missed the putt after the reception accorded by the crowd of 500 people assembled around the edge of the green. But Lloyd holed out." As a result he won by a single stroke over Willie Anderson.

Joe Lloyd, one of America's best players, was the winner of the 1897 U.S. Open.

Lloyd failed to defend the title in his own backyard at Myopia Hunt Club the following year, but he continued to compete with distinction for several years to come. His course record 68, shot at his home club in 1906, stood for many years. He remained the professional at Essex until 1909 when Donald Ross took over.

a day's acquaintance with the course it can readily be surmised that the nature of the test required for even fair golf was hard indeed. Still the narrow course and howling wind did not seem to bother the British ex-champion as he was equal to the emergency on every occasion," reported the *Boston Globe*.

Vardon began by taking the first two holes of the match and slowly built on that margin through the first round, leading 3 up at the break. When the wind was at his back, Vardon made two drives in excess of 275 yards, and his 77 established the new course record. He added to his lead early in the afternoon, but then the wind got the better of him. Three times it carried his ball off the course, and his opponents capitalized. "Joe Lloyd put up a grand game in the afternoon," noted the *Globe,* and after the local pair won the tenth hole they were only 2 down. The remaining holes were a comedy of errors. On the eleventh Vardon drove into a ditch and a fore-caddie picked up the ball, dropping it outside the hazard. Vardon unknowingly played from the dropped position, and his second shot was not allowed, "Consequently he gave up the hole, leaving the best ball 2-up on the afternoon's play." When Lloyd and Dingwall took the next hole the match was even.

Vardon won the fourteenth but lost the sixteenth when he "drove his ball out of the caddie's range of vision and it could not be found." He recovered on seventeen to reclaim a 1-up lead with one to go. "Everything depended on the last hole," wrote the *Globe.* All three got in screeching drives, with Lloyd having the greatest distance." On in three, Vardon missed a five-foot putt for a four, while Lloyd lay just 20 feet from the hole in two. "The spectators were fully convinced

The "Wee Drop" hole at Richmond County, a classic example of America's 1900 geometric style of design.

Spalding employee Tom Bendelow escorted Vardon on parts of his American tour.

that Lloyd would hole out in four, but his third went eight feet beyond the hole and his fourth stopped within two inches of the cup," so Vardon escaped with a 1-up victory.

The post-match buzz centered on J. H. Taylor's scheduled visit to Essex the following week, as the newspapers could not resist comparing the two men. Would he break Vardon's record? Playing under docile conditions on September 19, Taylor would merely equal Vardon's 77, and in the process lose to Lloyd and Dingwall 3 and 2.

Vardon's next match featured better weather and a flat, nearly treeless course on Staten Island, New York—probably a relief after the unfamiliar challenge of Essex. Richmond County Country Club was founded in 1888, the same year as St. Andrew's, but fox hunting and lawn tennis occupied the members until 1893, when the first golf holes were added. The club moved to a new site in 1897, and the nine original holes opened that year became eighteen the year after.

Vardon played two separate 18-hole matches. In the morning he found himself 1 down to Douglas Bonner, a member of the Princeton golf team, and his partner C. T. Stout, after the front nine. The Englishman squared the match on the eleventh, and "of the remaining seven holes he won five and only allowed his opponents to halve two," reported the *New York Times*. "He therefore finished 5-up on the round, making the low record of 75."

Vardon sliced another four strokes off that standard in the afternoon, posting 71 against Albert E. Paterson and John R. Chadwick, besting their combined efforts by seven strokes.

On September 18, Vardon was joined by Tom Bendelow for a trip to the Hartford Golf Club in central Connecticut. Bendelow served as caddie for the two 18-hole contests, a role he would reprise at the U.S. Open a few weeks later. Hartford was founded in 1896, and various short layouts that changed with the season gave way to a 5,350-yard, eighteen-hole routing in 1898. The course was built on

The clubhouse at the Hartford Golf Club in Connecticut.

The sixteenth green at Hartford.

clay and without professional guidance. Founder John Enders noted that "playing the course required agility, [and] the ability to climb post and rail fences and dodge cows." It was not the best course Vardon had seen, but probably not the worst either. According to Hartford's club history book, when asked about the quality of the layout, the Englishman offered, "Well sir, it's positively the worst course I have ever played on in my life." Given Vardon's even keel it is unlikely he made such a statement. Other accounts claim that Bendelow said, "I do not know what Harry thinks of it, but I think it is rotten."

Since throughout their careers both of these gentlemen went out of their way to not insult their hosts, it's a good bet that reporters

Looking out over the Hartford grounds.

created these quotes—and it would not have been the first time such stories were manufactured. In fact, the account of the match in the *Hartford Courant* makes no mention of such remarks, although the reporter himself stated, "the links had been softened somewhat by the rain, yet were not in their best condition," also calling them, "hard and rough." The only comment Vardon is credited with is that he "considers these links very difficult because of the unevenness of the ground and the fast greens."

Practice matches on the day prior to the official event pitted Vardon and Bendelow against H. S. Redfield and J. C. Stirling, a match the champion lost. The *Courant* described him as he appeared on the first tee the following morning: "His slender figure was clad in a pink striped shirt, without collar, sleeves rolled up, and in greenish drab knee breeches with stockings to match. His shoes were white canvas and he wore a brown cap." A dapper fellow for sure.

Club president Ralph W. Cutler teamed with Cooley versus Vardon.

Vardon played eighteen holes in the morning versus William Watson and James H. T. Brown, the club's greenkeeper from Scotland. In the afternoon he faced Ralph W. Cutler, the club president, and Frank R. Cooley, a founder and financier. More than five hundred people watched the games and Vardon won both by the same 3-and-2 margin. In the morning he also eclipsed the course record with a 70.

In 1900, Morris County Golf Club in Morristown, New Jersey, was one of America's finest courses, mentioned in the same breath as Chicago, Shinnecock, and Newport. Founded in 1894 by a group of women "of impeccable precedents," the club hosted the 1896 U.S. Women's Amateur and then the 1898 U.S. Amateur for the men. Taping at 5,960 yards, it was one of the country's longest and toughest, with the course record a 76 by Findlay Douglas.

Frank R. Cooley, one of the founders at Hartford, opposed Vardon in his match there.

Two practice matches were played on September 19: Vardon faced the best ball of James Tyng and John G. Bates in the morning, winning 4 and 2; and in the afternoon, partnered with Leland Garretson, he played in a foursome against Tyng and Bates, winning 3 and 2. Vardon lowered the course record by a stroke in the morning.

But the champion had his hands full on September 20, squaring off against the best ball of George Low of Dyker Meadow and Tom Hutchinson of Shinnecock. Though he played solid golf, Vardon found himself an incredible 11 down after eighteen. "Hutchinson probably never played more brilliantly in his life," raved the *Times*. "He got the seventh and eighth holes in three strokes each, 420 and 350 yards respectively." Hutchinson had two other 3s, made 5 on the 545-yard

A well-turfed layout was found at Morris County, one of America's best courses in 1900.

Teeing ground at Morris County.

thirteenth, and signed for a record 74. To put his exemplary performance in perspective, he shot 88 in the afternoon.

Vardon achieved a 78 in the afternoon, and by the time the thirty-
sixth green was reached he had whittled their lead down to four holes,
but the match was technically over at the 8-and-7 mark. The *Boston
Globe* was not kind: "Vardon had been set a very stiff task, but none
of those who believed he would be beaten
had any idea that his defeat would be so
thorough."

James Tyng opposed
Vardon at Morris County
Country Club.

J. H. Taylor was also on the East Coast at
this time, and according to some accounts
the New York papers had not treated him
with the same reverence as they had
Vardon. Editors were constantly trying to
trump up an animosity between the two
that didn't exist, and rumors were flying
about Taylor attending the Morris County
match. The British *Golf Illustrated* ran this
story on October 12: "It was stated that
'J. H. Taylor, the English Open Champion,
was on the course following the game in

Tom Hutchinson was an up-and-coming golfing star in the summer of 1900. Unfortunately his life was cut short by an equestrian accident later in the year.

disguise.' The amusing part of the matter was that as the afternoon paper containing this wonderful piece of news was selling in the streets, Taylor, who had been in New York all day, walked into the newspaper office and explained personally to the astonished editor that he was not also in Morristown, thirty-one miles away."

A tragic postscript to this match was the death of Thomas Hutchinson less than three months later. On December 11, 1900, at the winter estate of William C. Carnegie on Cumberland Island, Florida, where he was giving the Carnegie family golf lessons, Hutchinson was thrown from a horse and killed. He was just twenty-one years old and had moved from Scotland the previous March.

Over the Border

Vardon left the country for his next adventure. On Friday, September 21, he checked into the Queen's Hotel in Toronto and made it over to Rosedale for a quick afternoon practice round. Vardon played with Deighton Baxter, the club's secretary, as Cox hadn't arranged a practice match with the pro or for a member to host him. His thirty-six-hole game the following day was with George Lyon and Vere Brown, two of Canada's best professionals.

Canadian news sources were calling the event the most important in Canadian golf history. The club was selling badges to attend for

Vardon follows a tee ball at Rosedale in Toronto.

The flashy white shoes were occasionally part of Vardon's attire.

a dollar; at 4 A.M. a crew of men and horses was rolling and cutting the course by oil lamp; and delegations were attending from other Canadian courses.

For all the hype, only four hundred people showed up at the match, which Vardon won by 5 and 4, setting the course record with a 72. "From the tee, Vardon was no better than Lyon; or, at least, he was no longer, and not conspicuously straighter," wrote James Barclay in *Golf in Canada*. "But his shots to the green, his recovery shots when needed, his short approach shots, his holing of long putts over the lumpy greens—these are what won him the match and the

George Lyon was Canada's best player when he met Vardon at Rosedale in September.

Vardon tees off at Royal Montreal, North America's oldest golf club.

admiration of those who were witnesses to this entirely new way of playing the game."

In contrast to the second-class treatment he received at some of the finer American private clubs, Rosedale welcomed Vardon appropriately. "All in all, the day was such a triumph for the cause of golf, that Rosedale's president, Michael McLaughlin, threw a celebratory dinner that evening for Vardon and a select few at the National Club," according to the club's history book. "That event, at a time when golf pros weren't permitted to enter clubhouses, constituted an almost revolutionary instance of egalitarianism."

Three days later, the Montreal Stock Exchange closed early so that brokers could get to Royal Montreal in time for the afternoon match. Vardon had traveled from Toronto to Montreal with manager Cox and Tom Wall, Spalding's Canadian representative, and the excitement had come with them. Many of Canada's leading amateurs arrived early to see the match in preparation for the Canadian Amateur the following week.

Vardon played the best ball of pros George Cumming of Toronto Golf Club and Tom Smith of Royal Montreal in the morning, and despite a 77, lost by 1 up. In the afternoon he shaved six strokes off his score, set yet another course record, and won 5 and 4 against Montreal's two best amateurs, Percy Taylor and Gordon Macdougall.

It was widely reported afterward that Vardon panned the condition of the Canadian links in conversation with a magazine named *Saturday Night*. No direct quotes were offered, but the article added a sour note to what had been a pleasant sojourn. Vardon may not have realized how short the growing season and how deep the snow can be in Canada, or he may have never uttered an unkind word, and the whole affair could have been manufactured to incite the improvement of course conditioning in Canada. The truth is unknown. Vardon always made it a habit to read the news media, but he never dwelled on what they wrote. And when he packed his bags in Montreal and headed to Chicago he had only one thing on his mind: the upcoming U.S. Open.

CHAPTER 7

A Champion Once More

The Sixth U.S. Open

In 1900, the professional golfer competed in a vastly different arena than does today's pro. Nowadays, the top professional plays a long schedule of stroke-play tournaments, with the diversion of an occasional match-play event. A century ago it was just the opposite. After months of head-to-head match-play battles with the best players in America, Vardon arrived in Chicago for a medal-play contest with the national championship at stake.

Once again the media tried to create a controversy over Vardon's participation in the tournament. "Vardon's entry is problematic. His status as a competitor for the United States championship is entirely different from the other contestants, as Vardon is not employed by any recognized club, nor does he intend to make his domicile in this country," wrote the *New York Times*.

But the contingent of professionals who had befriended Vardon during his six months in the States came to his defense, citing the fact that the Open event was by definition accessible to all who wished to participate. Some suggested that a victory without Vardon in the field would be a hollow one, for the winner would not have defeated the best golfers in the country at the time of the championship.

Other news sources claimed that participation in the event was down because of the presence of Vardon and Taylor. True, entries had dropped by nearly a dozen from the previous year, but the 1899 tournament was conducted in Baltimore, a much easier locale for the largely East Coast–based contingent of professionals to get to than Chicago. Fewer amateurs also entered the event, and for good reason. Charles Blair Macdonald posted the low score among the amateurs, and his 355 was 42 strokes off the winning tally—and that on his home course, that he designed.

The truth is, no one shied away from the Open due to the presence of the English champions. More likely that presence was a magnet. Golfers wished to observe their technique and measure their own games against the best in the world. They also knew the pair would

The top golf professionals in America with Vardon (seated fourth from left) at the 1900 U.S. Open.

The full field at Chicago. Vardon is in the second row, fourth from the left, with Taylor to his left.

soon be gone and were not likely to return in short order. Furthermore, the Open in this era was a pleasant reunion where pros who emigrated from the Old Country got together, caught up with friends, and shared war stories over a wee nip of Scotch.

Vardon arrived in Wheaton on October 2, joining Taylor, who already had spent two days familiarizing himself with the layout. All the pros engaged in matches for their practice, a treat for the fans who arrived early. Vardon paired with Willie Norton in one, facing George Low and Alex Findlay before a large gallery.

Taylor pronounced the course the best he had seen in his three weeks in America, and one of the best inland courses anywhere. But the *Chicago Times Herald* made a less positive observation: "He had not had time to become acclimated, hardly time to forget that the toughly-rooted turf on an American course will not give way to a mashie as does the more easily persuaded turf of the old country links."

The golf course was in excellent condition, though some criticism was made regarding the greens. *Golf* magazine summarized by saying: "The grass was inclined to be a trifle wiry, and the mechanical brushing machines did not improve them. It was like a boy's head brushed the wrong way, and time and time again Taylor found all his calculations (particularly as to strength) upset by the resistance offered through the unsuspecting stiffness of the turf."

Vardon had left Chicago in July after several defeats and a misunderstanding regarding the tournament at Belmont. He had been blasted by the *Tribune* and was eager to make amends. "I was exceedingly keen to win the American Open Championship," Vardon wrote in *My Golfing Life,* "as I thought it would be a fitting climax to the successful tour which I had so far experienced. I felt that if I could add the American championship to my name, I would have accomplished everything which I had set out to try and do."

Vardon also wanted revenge for Taylor's victory in Scotland, while Taylor sought to become the first to hold both the American and British titles at the same time. Willie Smith looked to defend his title and prove himself equal to the English visitors. The stage was set.

"The championship took place in beautiful weather, and a large and fashionable crowd followed the players," Vardon wrote. Temperatures rose into the 70s, and a southerly breeze increased slightly every day. "President Thomas of the United States Golf Association said afterwards that it was the biggest crowd ever seen at a golf

The Spalding Prize

One month before the U.S. Open, Charles Cox sent a letter to the *Boston Globe*, a letter that was reprinted in other papers throughout the country: "It seems to be the general opinion that the playing of Harry Vardon and J. H. Taylor in the open championship may curtail the entries and possibly destroy the interest on the part of the resident professionals in the tournament. In order to serve as an inducement to them to enter, Mr. A. G. Spalding has cabled me to offer a purse of $150 and a $50 gold medal for the best score made by any player other than Vardon or Taylor."

An interesting gesture, but the editor of the *Chicago Tribune* quickly did the math: "The prize distribution already provides that the second player shall receive $150 and the third $125, and as the winner only gets $250 and a $50 gold medal the effect of Mr. Spalding's offer is to give to the home man more than that received by the winner. In other words, if Vardon and Taylor take first and second money neither will receive as much as the player who gets third place."

On October 2, USGA president W. B. Thomas issued a statement, saying in part, "The United States Golf Association does not sanction the offer and will take no official recognition of it. The Executive Committee was never asked if it would permit the award of this extra purse, and the first we knew of it was through the public announcements. When asked for my opinion, I had no hesitancy in telling the donors that I disapproved of it heartily, and that it was detrimental to the best interest of the tournament. Then the firm offered to withdraw the prize, but as many professionals had been led to enter in expectancy of winning extra money, I thought it would be unfair to them to call it off on the verge of the contest." Thomas thought the prize a dangerous precedent that the USGA would not sanction, and that in the future any such proposals should come through the national organization, not from private individuals.

David Bell, of Midlothian Country Club, who shot 323, ten strokes behind champion Vardon, was the third-place finisher and according to all accounts won $125. There were no further mentions of the Spalding bonus in the local or national press.

game in America. Although the gallery was very enthusiastic, they were extremely well controlled, and did not in any way interfere with the players."

Vardon was paired with Willie Smith, and, unlike the procedure used today, the two would remain so throughout the four rounds.

John Henry Taylor

Always known as J. H. Taylor, the English lad grew up caddieing at Westward Ho! near his home in Northam and also was engaged as "boot boy" in the house of General Hutchinson, "so to me fell the privilege of shining Horace's shoes." His victory in the 1893 Open Championship was the first by a non–Scottish-born player, and not very popular among the professional golfers. Taylor backed it up by defending his title the following year, eventually winning the Claret Jug five times.

Despite press reports to the contrary, Vardon and Taylor were friends with deep respect for each other. For many years their games were perfectly matched; each won his share of events, and a close and well-played battle was guaranteed whenever they met.

Taylor, from a series of cards issued in 1900.

Taylor came to America in August of 1900 and followed in Vardon's footsteps, competing in the U.S. Open and playing matches throughout the East and Midwest. It's unclear why the two never played against each other in the United States, but accusations and innuendo flew for months over the issue, mostly fueled by reporters desperate to see the champions clash. Taylor returned to England in early October for a tournament at Mid-Surrey Golf Club, where he was the professional, and he was impressed with America. "I found the standard of play over here much higher than I expected," he told the *New York Times*, "and I consider the links of the Chicago Golf Club the best I have visited."

Taylor posted a 76 in the opening round, and it looked as though Vardon would be just two back as he stood over a short putt at the eighteenth. "Vardon actually missed the ball itself in making a short putt, and was quite as much astonished as any of the spectators at the phenomenon," reported *Golf*. "Taylor's explanation is that there must have been an unusually thick bunch of this stiff grass just back of the ball, and that it actually prevented the putter blade from going through. How else can one account for the astonishing fact that Harry Vardon failed by a good two inches to hit his ball, and on the putting green at that?"

Crowds follow play at the 1900 U.S. Open.

Three back after the first round, Vardon rallied in the afternoon and stood 1 up over Taylor at the conclusion of the afternoon play. They were already distancing themselves from the rest of the field as David Bell, in third place, stood five strokes off the lead. "In the third round I played exceedingly good golf, and with a score of 76 to Taylor's 79, led the field by four shots. Thus, with eighteen holes to be played, I found myself in an extremely strong position. It was only necessary for me to play steady golf in my last round to win the championship," Vardon recalled.

He did just that, posting an 80 in a strong wind. Only two players did better, and others did far worse; Walter Egan of Onwentsia struggled to a 102. With the wind sweeping across the line of play, Vardon finished in style. "His very last full shot of the tournament was typical of his style at its best," reported *Golf*—"a beautiful brassey of something over 200 yards that came straight for the flag and stopped on the far edge of the green." A pair of putts, and Vardon had won the U.S. Open by two over Taylor. Bell was the leading American, nine strokes back.

"Needless to say, I was delighted to have won the title of American Open Champion, and the reception which I received at the conclusion of the big event could not, in any way, have been more sincere if the victory had been gained by an American player," Vardon wrote.

The champion sinks the final putt on the eighteenth green for a
two-stroke victory over J. H. Taylor.

"Taylor did not complain," reported the *Times Herald*. "He took his
defeat as a good loser should, congratulated the winner, and allowed
that Vardon played the better golf." Vardon could now continue his
trip without the constant moniker of former Open champion.

A Golfing Pilgrim

On his way back to Massachusetts, Vardon stopped at the Country
Club of Scranton in Pennsylvania, where the club was about to conduct its annual amateur tournament for the Scranton Cup. The club
had been founded in 1896 with a nine-hole course designed by Tom
Bendelow, to which Tom Gourlay added another nine holes in 1898.
The two nines together traversed a total of only 4,273 yards. Surpris-
ingly, Vardon's best score in two trips around the links was 70, one
more than the course record. Still, the newly crowned champion
beat the best ball of A. Z. Huntington and Thomas H. Watkins in
the morning and club captain John H. Brooks and T. C. Fuller in the
afternoon by identical scores of 2 and 1 in eighteen-hole matches.
"Harry Vardon must now be styled the open champion of the United
States instead of the former champion of Great Britain," admitted
the *New York Times* in reporting on the game.

Rumors of Vardon's remaining schedule continued to circulate as
they had throughout the tour. In mid-October, the *Times* claimed that
"after finishing his golf dates in the East [Vardon] will start for the
Pacific Coast where dates have already been arranged at Monterey,

A green at the Country Club of Scranton.

Pasadena, San Francisco, San Diego, and Los Angeles." Those dates may have been talked about with pros from the Northeast, several of whom were now taking winter jobs on the West Coast, but no mention of them was made in any of Vardon's writings, schedules, or interviews.

Clearly the champion was growing tired of being on the road. It had been four months since he left home, already as long as his earlier absence. He missed the simplicity of his role as a club pro, the serenity of his home life, and his friendly countrymen. But those pleasures were far from the routine of his traveling life in the States. For American golf fans, eager to see how their new Open champion would fare, their focus was his October 13 date at Brae Burn and a rematch with Bernard Nicholls.

Thus far in his tour of America, Harry Vardon had played more than sixty-five matches and had lost fifteen, but he had been defeated only once head to head by a single player. And that was Nicholls, on a grassless golf course in Florida eight months previous. Now they met on a fall day in New England over the three-year-old, 2,741-yard, nine-hole course in West Newton, Massachusetts.

Nicholls captured the first hole of the match, but Vardon assumed a two-hole lead after the first nine. Nicholls rallied on the second loop and stood 1 up at lunch. It was the same in the afternoon, with each player taking brief leads only to find the match back to

The original Brae Burn clubhouse.

A large gallery at Brae Burn watches Vardon putt during his
second defeat by Bernard Nicholls.

square. The *Boston Globe* reported that luck seemed to be against
Vardon, as "time and again he had the misfortune to rim the cup on
his putts." But the *New York Times* was less charitable, stating that
Vardon "was off in his putting, and he missed a number of short
putts at critical points in the game." For Nicholls, on the other hand,
"it was a common occurrence for him to run down putts averaging
from 4 to 12 feet."

Vardon kept himself in the contest with his long game—and they
came to eighteen all square. But there the champion choked. "Vardon
had the honor at the last hole and sliced his ball into the long grass
fifteen yards away," reported the *Times*. "He had a poor lie, and in

Bernard Nicholls at the finish of his swing.

trying to get out dug up the turf and made about 70 yards. Nicholls' drive was a beautiful one. He was on the green in 2 against 3 for his opponent."

Nicholls third shot was dead to the hole, and, according to the *Globe,* "He laid a half stymie for Vardon, and when the latter made a fine try for the hole he struck Nicholls' ball and lost the match, as Nicholls went down on his fourth." The *Globe* summarized by adding, "All in all, Nicholls outclassed the champion on the greens, and that tells the story of the defeat in a nutshell."

How did Nicholls defeat Vardon a second time? Clearly, he was not intimidated, nor did he allow all the hype to take him from his game. He could almost keep up with Vardon off the tee, did not destroy his chances with wayward approaches, and putted far better. And although one could dismiss his first win as a fluke on a 1,800-yard "parlour course," even the British *Golf Illustrated* admitted that "Nicholls has never been considered exactly a front-rank man, but it is evident that he must be a match-player of more than average merit to win two matches in one year against such a man as Vardon."

Vardon, of course, had nothing to say, leaving that to his agent. "Mr. Cox, Vardon's manager, said that Nicholls had played a superior short game, which accounted for the defeat of the champion," according to the *Globe*. For the Englishman it was simply on to the next engagement.

Oakley Country Club in Watertown was established in February of 1898 as the Cambridge Golf and Country Club, changing its name later that same year. Willie Campbell planned the original nine-hole course, which was expanded to a 5,850-yard, eighteen-hole layout by Donald Ross, shortly after his arrival from Scotland in 1899. Ross continued to work on the course during his brief tenure at Oakley and held the course record of 74 when Vardon arrived.

October 16 was an excellent day for golf, and a crowd of three hundred members and invited guests arrived for a thirty-six-hole match, with Vardon playing the best ball of Alex Findlay and Donald Ross. Although the fame of Ross would spread rapidly in the years to come, he was not a well-known figure in American golf at the time—as is witnessed by the fact that in recounting Vardon's tour, the *1901 Spalding Golf Guide* listed him as "Duncan" Ross.

"The course was in good condition, thanks to the endeavors of the green committee, and the sun's rays did much toward making the turf suitable for good rolls," reported the *Globe*. Though Ross received no credit for his architectural or greenkeeping abilities, he was cited for his good play: "Ross gained many admirers for his fine game, his approaching being very accurate. He drove well, too, and after the first few holes succeeded in getting admirable direction."

Ross received little help from Findlay in the morning round but managed to stay close to the champion, despite some nervous jitters on the first few holes. On the opening hole Ross sliced his tee ball into a mud patch and had to take a drop, then pulled his second into a stone wall. On the second hole he sliced his approach onto a nearby roadway, and on the third green he picked up his ball after three putts. Despite the miscues, the challengers were only 2 down after the first nine holes, and Ross turned his game around on the inward half, keeping Vardon to only 3 up after eighteen.

In the afternoon, "Ross drove some very long balls and his putting was a feature of the match," noted the *Globe*. Findlay also recovered from a morning malaise during which "he had the misfortune to slice and pull his ball quite frequently. He steadied down, however, as the

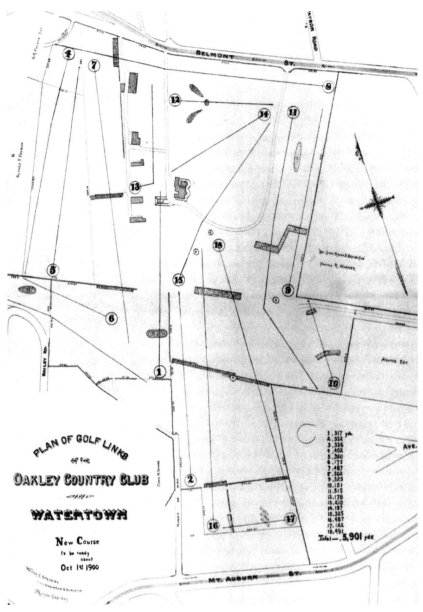

Vardon was one of the earliest players to test the first golf course
designed by Ross in America.

Donald Ross

Donald Ross arrived in America in April of 1899 and set to work at the Oakley Country Club on 400-foot-high Strawberry Hill overlooking downtown Boston and its harbor. The primitive Willie Campbell–designed golf course he inherited was cramped, poorly drained, and built on rocks and clay. His job was to redesign it for Robert Wilson, an astronomy professor at Harvard and charter member of the club whom he had met in Dornoch, Scotland. The Ross course was to be ready by October 1, 1900—and little did he know at the time that one of the early players on the links would be Harry Vardon. Of the challenge he faced at the Oakley course Ross later wrote, "It looked like an impossible problem. But I went to work on it with fifty men and that year I sent $2,000 home to my mother in Dornoch."

Donald Ross had been in the United States for a year and a half when he met Vardon at Oakley.

Ross's later career is well documented, including his nearly fifty years at Pinehurst, some four hundred course designs, and a lasting impact on golf in America. But in 1900, he was a young clubmaker, teaching professional, and greenkeeper who was pleased to be in America. In the early years, Ross was quite a player, winning the Massachusetts Open in 1905 and 1911 and placing fifth in the U.S. Open in 1903.

match wore on, and in the afternoon was playing in his old form again." Vardon did not eclipse the course record Ross had established, but he closed the match on the thirteenth green by 6 and 5.

Two days later, Vardon appeared at Merrimack Valley Country Club in Lawrence, Massachusetts, a course Ross would remodel ten years later. Established in 1898, "The club has a nine-hole course of 2,422 yards, and is said to be one of the finest in New England," according to *Harper's Official 1900 Golf Guide.* Alex Findlay joined the Englishman on a day when the wind had "the tendency to send the

The Merrimack Valley clubhouse in Lawrence, Massachusetts.

high drives out of the course at times," as described in the *Boston Globe.*

Findlay and Vardon had become fast friends during their nine months together. Besides Charles Cox, Findlay had spent more time with Vardon than anyone, traveling with him, lodging next to him, and playing more golf against him than anyone. Not counting practice matches, this was the fifteenth time they had squared off, and Findlay had been successful as part of a best-ball team on several occasions. With his brother at Maplewood, with Arthur Fenn at Poland Spring, and with Horace Rawlins at Waumbek, Findlay had come out on top—but he had yet to beat the champion solo.

It seemed that those laurels would be his at Merrimack Valley. "Findlay played in good form," wrote the *Globe,* "his approaches and putting being very clever." The challenger led by a hole after the morning round, and when Vardon missed a four-foot putt on the second hole of the afternoon the margin had doubled. It doubled again before twenty-seven holes had been completed, and Vardon could knock only one from Findlay's column, shortly thereafter.

"With Findlay 3-up and three to play it certainly seemed that the Englishman would lose, but undaunted he drove for the seventh hole.

Vardon attracts a crowd, and police protection, as he tees off at
Fall River Country Club.

Vardon's driving had improved much, while the reverse was true of
Findlay's," reported the *Globe*. Vardon captured seven and eight to
bring the match to the thirty-sixth hole. "The enthusiasm ran high as
the men began the play for the ninth hole. Vardon made one of his
usual drives, while Findlay fell short of 100 yards. The hole went to
Vardon in three, necessitating an extra hole, which the Englishman
won." Although it was not the last time the two would battle, being
dormie three, it was Findlay's best chance to unseat his friend, and
it blew away in the west wind.

On October 20, the curtain went up on the next act at Fall River
Country Club in southern Massachusetts. Findlay and Fenn teamed up
to take on Vardon and club member R. M. Hawkins on the nine-hole,
2,490-yard layout that *Harper's Golf Guide* called "somewhat stony
in places, with greens capable of improvement." The Fenn-designed
course was just a year old, and "Groundsman Jack Howard had the
greens in the best possible shape," considering he had been hired
merely a month earlier.

"As a social feature the day was a great success," noted the *Fall
River Daily Herald*. "During the interval between morning and afternoon play, Sokoll served light refreshments in a marquee near the
clubhouse, while within the house a blazing fire on the hearth made

it cozy for those that rested there. Lieutenant Milton and a squad of patrolmen from the North station kept the heights against trespassers without credentials." Vardon established another course record with a pair of 74s, and his team prevailed 3 and 2.

Vardon and Findlay stayed in the area for another game on October 23, this time at the Hawthorne Golf Club in New Bedford. A short course barely two years old, Hawthorne had greens that proved challenging: "Both players had their troubles on the greens and their approach shots stopped short on the heavy turf," reported the *Globe*. "They missed putts that looked easy, and Vardon found it difficult to drop the ball in the hole several times when it lay less than a yard away."

The champion parlayed a second trip around into a course record of 32, but their first tour was a different story: "Neither Vardon or Findlay played better than amateur golf on the first round, and both had cards of 41." Findlay struggled to a 79 and 76, offering Vardon a 7-and-6 victory.

Vesper Country Club on Tyngs Island outside of Lowell, Massachusetts, is a most interesting property. The organization began as the Vesper Boat Club in 1875 with most activities centered on the Merrimack River surrounding the island home of the club. On the mainland, members also established the Lowell Country Club in 1892, and after a golf demonstration by Essex County professional Joe Lloyd in 1895 installed a six-hole course on the island. Later that year the course was expanded to nine holes, and in the fall of 1896, Alex Findlay expanded and formalized the circuit. Eventually the two entities were combined to form the Vesper Country Club.

The architect of the golf course accompanied the champion to the island. According to Vesper's club history: "The big event of 1900 was when Harry Vardon, the British champion, came for exhibitions at Vesper, played 18 holes with Alex Findlay October 24, spent the night tenting on the island, and the next day played a 36-hole match with the Vesper pro, John Harland. He gave a brilliant exhibition, lowering the course record and winning both matches."

Findlay's near-miss versus Vardon at Merrimack Valley a week earlier was now a distant memory—the champion dominated him at Vesper, winning 13 and 12. It was one of those rare rounds where Vardon's putting matched the rest of his performance. Members hoped their own pro could offer stiffer resistance. "It was a gala day for the Vesper members and a large gallery of enthusiasts witnessed the play," reported the *Globe*. "Vardon's wonderful playing of Wednes-

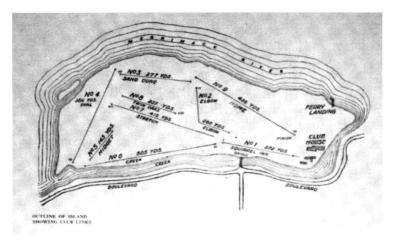

The unique Vesper layout occupied an island in the Merrimack River.

day brought out the golfers in force and they gave the victor a hearty greeting. It was ideal weather, as there was no wind to speak of, and the course was in good condition."

Vardon's morning 83 was not his best effort, though it left him with a 3-up advantage. He shaved five strokes in the afternoon for another course record and a 6-and-5 win. By the evening he had departed the Bay State after successful games at six clubs. When he returned thirteen years later it ended in an historic encounter with a young caddie named Francis Ouimet at the Country Club in Brookline.

Home Stretch

Not being familiar with the weather in the Northeast, Vardon probably didn't realize he was testing his luck by agreeing to play in late October. His education began at the Albany Country Club in New York state. "Worse weather for a golf match could hardly be imagined than that at Albany on Vardon's visit there," recounted *Golf Illustrated*. "A heavy cold rain pelted the players, and pools of water had formed all over the course, even on the greens, so that accurate putting was in consequence most difficult."

On October 26, Vardon played an eighteen-hole practice match against Harry R. Sweney, the club's amateur champion, beating him 70 to 79 and lowering the course record by five shots. The nine-hole course had been in use since 1894, though A. Ricketts had

Vardon stripes a tee ball at Albany Country Club in New York.

Organizers had hoped for a day like this for Vardon's visit to
Albany Country Club, but instead it was cold and rainy.

The Albany layout included many interesting features.

improved it considerably a year after its installation.

For the main match on the 27th, Vardon opposed John Reid Jr., son of the founder of New York's St. Andrew's, who was now the venerable club's captain. Amateur Reid had two professional partners for his 36-hole encounter with Vardon: George Pierson joined him in the morning and Valentine Fitzjohn in the afternoon. "The Albany people speak in the highest terms of the playing, and give Mr. Fitzjohn, the representative of the Otsego Golf Club, many compliments on his work," said an Albany newspaper. "The latter drives an unusually low ball that has a long run on it, and these terrific shots captured the gallery."

A group of three hundred intrepid golf fans from clubs throughout the capi-

John Reid Jr., son of the founder of Saint Andrew's, played with two separate partners against Vardon at Albany.

tal region slogged around the property following the game and were impressed with Fitzjohn's length and Reid's short game. But Vardon prevailed by 4 and 3—his reward being a warm Pullman car for the transit back to New York City.

The Albany Country Club's amateur champion and golf writer
Harry Sweney demonstrates a follow-through technique.

Vardon and Cox took a few days of rest back in New York, reflecting on the trip thus far, enjoying the night life, and relaxing. There were six matches left, some involving a trip to Colorado, and it was hoped the champion would sail home before the holidays.

Colonel F. L. Denny and C. J. Bell of the Chevy Chase Club just outside of Washington, D.C., in Maryland had arranged for a Vardon visit on November 3 to play the best ball of Donald Ball, professional at the Washington Golf Club and their own pro, Willie Tucker. They were making the game available to the public and charging a one-dollar admission price to both members and guests.

The Chevy Chase Club already was one of the premier sporting establishments in the country. Home club to many of the nation's leading politicians, judges and public figures, Chevy Chase featured polo, tennis, fox and hounds, and an eighteen-hole golf course. The well-turfed layout was established in November of 1898, laid out by Willie Davis and Willie Tucker.

Vardon arrived a day early and was greeted by club officials and brought to the property. He played a morning round by himself and

Willie Tucker

Willie Tucker Sr. was part of the first wave of British golf professionals to emigrate to America in the 1800s. He was born in 1871 in Redhill, Surrey, England, where his father was a greenkeeper at the Wimbledon Common golf course. As a teenager Tucker worked with Tom Dunn on projects in England, France, and Switzerland; the Dunn family ran the most active golf course construction business in the world. In 1895, his brother Samuel convinced him to come to America and join him as co-professional at St. Andrew's in New York.

Tucker, one of the few competent course designers working in America during the late 1890s, produced layouts for Philadelphia Cricket Club in 1895, the Springhaven Club in Wallingford, Pennsylvania, and Maidstone Club on Long Island in 1896,

Willie Tucker (*in doorway*) with an assistant at his shop at Saint Andrew's, before moving south.

and a new (and the present) site for St. Andrew's in 1897. Tucker continued to design dozens of courses throughout the country, eventually retiring to Albuquerque, New Mexico, where he planned a course for the University of New Mexico in 1941. Tucker was also a respected turfgrass expert who disseminated information on soils, grass varieties, and maintenance techniques in the early decades of course management.

Tucker learned his golf under Willie Dunn Jr. when they were together at Biarritz in France in 1888. Never one of the top players in the United States, he entered the Open for four consecutive years starting in 1896. After finishing 36 strokes behind champion Willie Smith in 1899 he gave up his goal of winning a major event.

delivered a record 73 on his first look. In the afternoon he teamed with Ormsby McCammon, one of the club's top amateurs, and played a foursome match against F. Oden Hortsman and his own manager, Charles Cox. Vardon and McCammon won 5 up over eighteen holes.

The clubhouse at the Chevy Chase Club outside of Washington, D.C.

While the *Washington Post* claimed that "Vardon's wonderful drives astonished the Washington golf players who watched," the paper also noted that, "there are many club members who believe that the pair [Ball and Tucker] will manage to defeat the Open American champion."

Not many were there to find out the following day. "Owing to a steady rain only about fifty persons witnessed the game," noted the *New York Times*. "The match had been well advertised and had been looked forward to with great interest by all the golf lovers in the city," added the *Post*. "Notwithstanding the rain, the experts were there, and by the breathless and unflagging interest with which they followed the players through the driving showers, they proved themselves a most enthusiastic and appreciative audience." The reporter added that five women were added to the crowd in the afternoon, and that they "trailed bravely through the wet grass, following the play as closely and with apparently as much interest as the men."

Vardon stood 1 up at the halfway point, but the highlight of the day came on the seventh hole of the afternoon round. "From the seventh tee Vardon made a sensational drive, sending the ball almost to the second bunker," reported the *Post*. "The drive was about 265 yards, and was the longest ever made on this hole." Winning the hole was part of his domination of the first nine holes of the afternoon, and the local pros were unable to recover. Vardon closed them out on the thirteenth hole by 6 and 5. And to make amends for the poor attendance due to the rotten weather he agreed to return in two weeks for another game.

The clubhouse at Fairfield County Golf Club.

On November 6, 1900—a day on which Americans re-elected President William McKinley, only to see him assassinated in office ten months later—Vardon played at the Fairfield County Golf Club in southern Connecticut. The club had been organized in 1895 with a nine-hole layout of 2,770 yards, and, as *Harper's Golf Guide* noted, "The members of this club are very energetic, and they maintain an excellent nine-hole course." His opponent was the former U.S. Amateur champion and club member Findlay Douglas. Although the weather was better, the competition was not as Douglas "did not come quite up to his game, and was beaten by 10 up and 8 to play," according to the *Times*. Vardon opened a sizeable lead with 40 and 41 in the morning; and another 40 to start the afternoon round was all he needed.

The Apawamis Club in Rye, New York, was the next stop for Vardon on November 10. The Club was already on its third layout in 1900, having started with nine holes in 1896 at the Anderson farm, moved to the Jib farm in 1897, and found its permanent home in 1899. Willie Dunn had assisted member Maturin Ballou in planning the first eighteen-hole layout, and it was Ballou who teamed with golf professional Willie F. Davis to confront Vardon. It was another rout, with the champion going up by four in the morning and finishing the duo off by 7 and 6 in the afternoon.

At the conclusion of his match, Vardon returned to the clubhouse to find he had been robbed. Someone had entered the building, gained access to a room upstairs where Vardon had left his waistcoat,

William F. Davis

The singular professional who set a pattern that hundreds would follow was Willie Davis of Hoylake, England. Davis came to Royal Montreal in 1881, but a dispute with club founder and president Alexander Dennistoun over his greenkeeping duties ended the relationship abruptly, and he returned to work at Carnoustie. Davis made the journey to North America for good in 1889, spending time at Royal Montreal, planning a twelve-hole design for Shinnecock Hills, and then arriving at Newport Country Club in time to prepare the course for the first USGA championships in 1895. Despite the pressures of hosting the tournament, Davis placed fifth in the inaugural Open; and in subsequent playings regularly finished in the top twenty.

Willie Davis was one of best liked and most highly respected pros in America.

As early as 1898, Davis split his time between Newport in the summer and the Washington Golf Club in Arlington, Virginia, for the winter, before accepting a full-time position at Apawamis in New York in 1900. Davis was frequently invited to tournaments and challenge matches, being well liked by his peers.

In January of 1902, friends and colleagues were shocked when Davis, at age thirty-nine, contracted pneumonia and died a week later. A funeral service in New York was attended by many of his brethren before he was buried in Montreal.

rifled through his pockets and removed several items of value, both monetary and sentimental. His cash had not been touched, but a watch, chain, and charms were gone.

The gold watch was studded with diamonds; the chain and charms had been presented to him by English nobility. "I'd give $100 for their return," Vardon told the newspapers. "The watch was given to me by the Jersey Golf Club of the Isle of Jersey. The chain

The bunkers at the Apawamis Club had a natural look, unlike many
American courses of the day. Vardon thought the Apawamis
course was one of the best he played.

A fully grassed green at Apawamis in Rye, New York.

was given me by the Scarborough Golf Club of England." The *Times*
claimed their value to be $1,000; there is no record of them having
been recovered.

Vardon's final appearance in the New York metropolitan area
was a grand public affair at Van Cortlandt Park. The event began
on November 15 at Carnegie Hall, where Vardon was the guest of

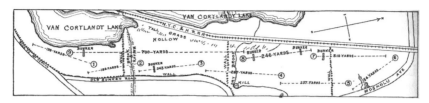

Van Cortlandt Park was one of the few public courses Vardon played during his year in America.

Unique hazards at Van Cortlandt.

honor at "the first social event ever held by the club." Awards for the season were presented—"a glittering array of silver sups and medallions"—followed by musical entertainment for the three hundred assembled guests.

Other than a few resort courses such as Poland Spring and Pinehurst, Vardon's golf had been confined to the private clubs of America—not surprising considering that nearly every course in 1900 was private, and that the $250 fee he commanded was beyond the budget of the few public venues that did exist. But Van Cortlandt in New York City was different, with enough affluent supporters to raise by subscription the stipend required.

On November 17, Vardon faced the city's professional, Valentine Flood, who paired with two different amateurs in eighteen-hole matches. "Being on Saturday, the game drew a large crowd in the afternoon, fully 3,000 people being present, requiring a large force of police to keep the course clear," announced the special American correspondent to the British *Golf Illustrated*. Even if the crowd estimate is a slight exaggeration (the *New York Times* did suggest about

Valentine Flood

One of the seminal figures in early American golf—who somehow managed to fly under the radar, even to most historians—Val Flood introduced many innovations and made his mark on important courses in a long distinguished career that continued into the 1940s. Flood arrived from his native Australia in 1893, finding a job at the Halcyon Hall Golf Links in Millbrook, New York, where he remained until 1897. The two years following he was the pro at the Country Club of Pittsfield in Massachusetts, moving to Van Cortlandt Park in 1900.

Valentine Flood came to America from Australia and held a number of high-profile posts in the early decades of the twentieth century.

As an employee of the New York City park system, Flood had a devil of a time putting the links at Van Cortlandt and Pelham Park into condition, though the results of his labors were celebrated by the *New York Times* in June of 1900: "Val Flood, the new Van Cortlandt Park golf professional, is to be congratulated on having put the course in such admirable condition." In addition to his agronomic talents, Flood "has made some very beneficial changes in regard to caddies ... bringing order out of former chaos and noise." He also instituted a system of starting times, made and repaired clubs, organized regular competitions for golfers of all talent levels, and attempted to bring a private-club aura to the most public of links.

Flood seldom competed on a national scale but continued to play golf into his senior years. From 1911 to 1913 he served the Woodstock Country Club in Vermont and then began a twenty-seven-year affiliation with Shuttle Meadow Country Club in Connecticut. In 1938, on his seventieth birthday, Flood shot 75 and 76 at his home club in an era when virtually no one was able to shoot their age.

five hundred less), it was still the largest crowd of the tour. "If any further justification of the popularity of golf were needed it was given once and for all yesterday," stated the *Times*. "The beauty of it was that with few exceptions Vardon was entirely new to his audience, but the enthusiasm was as keen and the appreciation of sterling plays as well judged as could be seen at any of the big clubs which Vardon has honored with his presence."

Offering a classic illustration of Murphy's Law, the *Times* reported that "The greens have never been worse this season. The greens were fearfully heavy, and the beauty of witnessing a cleverly run-up putt was entirely lacking." By now, Vardon must have grown accustomed to the miserable greens of America. He had started in the clay of Laurence Harbor, and ten months later little had changed.

Amateur William Freeland had the honor of joining Flood against Vardon in the morning; the secretary and captain of Van Cortlandt, William C. Morrill, took his spot in the afternoon. Neither fared very well playing the master before thousands of fans—and who can blame them? The forenoon group won only two holes of the eighteen, losing by five overall. The late contingent also managed two wins, but one came on the last hole when Vardon drove into a pond and picked up as "it got so dark at this time that it was difficult to watch the game." The final tally found Vardon 7 up after eighteen.

A week later Vardon fulfilled his promise to return to the Chevy Chase Club. Though it did not pour as it had for the earlier visit, the ground was thoroughly saturated, offering no roll or opportunities for sharp scoring. The conditions did not stop Vardon from setting a new course record of 72 in the afternoon, and he needed every stroke as Tucker and Ball put forth a stout challenge. Actually Ball did most of the heavy lifting as Tucker took sick before the game and had little to contribute. Vardon claimed the sixteenth hole in the afternoon for a 1-up lead and held on through the last two holes to maintain that slim margin of victory.

Final Fling

Given the inaccuracies that existed in the reporting of Vardon's schedule throughout his visit, it's hard to know whether games had been arranged in California or not. And if they had, did they fall through due to a lack of financial resources on the part of the clubs, or had Vardon grown tired of his endless journey and felt the homing instinct? He had communicated with Willie Smith and David Bell, who had committed to visit the West Coast, but on November 28, the *New York Times* reported that "Vardon is evidently disappointed in not being able to reach the Pacific Coast, but that plan had to be abandoned because a sufficiently large number of clubs was not obtained to pay the price." Though the synopsis seems credible, the paper suggested later in the same article that Vardon would return to the United States in the spring and "settle here permanently," when he had no such plans.

It was also suggested that Vardon would play return engagements around Thanksgiving at both Essex County Club and Vesper Country Club in Massachusetts, but as the winter weather closed in the clubs backed out. He did have one more trip on his agenda, and it involved one of his longest excursions yet. Tom Bendelow was along for this extravaganza as well.

"Harry Vardon will make a flying trip to Colorado before sailing for home December 15," stated the *Times*. Given that the Wright Brothers' escapade at Kitty Hawk was still three years away, "flying" did not denote hopping on a commercial airliner. Rather it referred to one of the express trains that traversed the country without stopping at every small-town platform. It was still an expensive and time-consuming undertaking for a single golf game. "The Denver Golf Club has been trying for some time to get Vardon for an exhibition match, but he refused to make so long a trip for one game," noted the *Times*. "The golf club at Colorado Springs recently requested a Vardon match, and C. S. Cox said yesterday that plans had been perfected to leave the city for Denver on Monday."

Vardon had enjoyed his time in the Adirondacks and the White Mountains, but nothing could prepare him for the grandeur of the Rocky Mountains. "I had a most enjoyable time in Denver and Colorado Springs," Vardon wrote. "The scenery there was magnificent, and the air extremely strong. In fact so strong was the air, that on several occasions it caused my nose to bleed."

There are not many accounts of Vardon's recreation during his year in America, but he does offer this account of Colorado: "While in this part of the country, I engaged in some wild duck hunting. I remember, on one occasion, going out in the evening with a friend after wild duck. He was an extremely good shot. He told me if I took the first bird he would take the second. I fully intended to carry out his instructions. It is now many years ago, but I remember quite well although shooting at the first I brought down the second bird. I came to the conclusion after this exhibition that I was a much better shot with a golf club than with a gun."

Vardon's host at the Overland Park Club in Denver was Walter Fairbanks, and the two played a practice match on December 7. Fairbanks was an amateur champion, both at the club and in regional

Walter Fairbanks brought Vardon to Colorado and played against him in practice and a match at Overland Park.

The first tee at Overland Park in Denver, Colorado.

The irrigation ditch at Overland Park figured prominently in the play and maintenance of the layout.

golf tournaments, but he convinced Vardon to give him half a stroke per hole, and Fairbanks won 4 and 3 over eighteen holes. Local knowledge helped, for the course had some unusual features.

By means of a large irrigation ditch the club had diverted water from the mountain-fed Platte River nearby. Traveling through underground pipe below the Club's two horseracing tracks, the water flowed throughout the course in waterways whose banks acted as bunkers and hazards. Larger channels bordering fairways served as reservoirs, while smaller streams nestled close to greens. In an article titled *Golf in Colorado,* S. H. Thompson Jr. wrote: "Eastern players who visit the club in the morning with the intention of playing later, must experience a feeling of despair as they watch the groundkeepers calmly perforate the canal in numerous places, till the links becomes a veritable swamp. But that thirsty soil, which does not get more than a month of natural moisture during the entire year, drinks up the water with the voracity of a sponge, leaving the turf in excellent condition for the afternoon play." The author called it "the highest state of man's handiwork."

Keeping the ball out of the canals was what was needed from the golfer, and Vardon's practice round on the 2,709-yard, nine-hole layout had prepared him well. On December 9, by 3 and 2, he defeated the best ball of three players: club professional James Russell, Fairbanks, and member Frank L. Woodard.

After the match, Vardon, Cox, and Bendelow proceeded south to Colorado Springs for a date at the Town and Gown Club, and it seems

The Town and Gown clubhouse in Colorado Springs.

It was fitting that Vardon's final stop featured grassless greens similar to the ones he played early in his trip in Florida.

fitting that the final course he played bore a striking resemblance to some of the first courses he played in Florida. Established in 1894, and boasting an eighteen-hole, 6,095-yard course for 250 members, Town and Gown was flourishing, but Thompson described the golf course thus: "The club has been content with a course laid out on a rolling prairie, which knows not the benefits of irrigation. There are some extenuating circumstances that might be presented as an excuse for the club, namely that the grounds are some distance from the city waterworks and the plane of the course is above the level of the irrigating ditches." In other words, Town and Gown had about as much grass on it as Ormond Beach.

Vardon's final day was practically ignored by the press as none of the major papers followed him west. He played two eighteen-hole matches, beating the club professional W. W. Campbell and amateur H. B. Davis by 3 and 2 in the morning; and defeating Davis and club president W. K. Jewett by 1 up in the afternoon. And with that, his amazing year was over.

CHAPTER 8

One Year in a Long Career

Harry Vardon, Charles Cox, and Tom Bendelow "flew" back to New York in time to attend an end-of-the-year get-together of the East Coast golf professionals. Vardon originally had planned to leave for England on December 15, but the trip to Colorado had delayed that, and the reunion of golf pros had been postponed to accommodate his schedule. The party at Hotel Hungaria in Union Square was a festive affair as the pros caught up on the year's events and related their winter plans in southern climates. "Vardon has been asked to attend and bid his resident countrymen in this land farewell," according to the *New York Times*.

There were many rumors and a wealth of inaccurate statements regarding his future. "Harry Vardon, the great British golf expert, has decided to make his home in the United States," claimed the *Los Angeles Times*. "He will visit England this winter to close up his affairs preparatory to leaving the country for good. He says there is more money to be made here in golf than in Great Britain."

The American correspondent for *Golf Illustrated* added, "Accounts of what Vardon will do in the future, mostly of contradictory nature, appear in the papers nearly every day. The most probable tale is that he intends to settle in this country as professional to one of the leading clubs, carrying on a club business in addition. It is said that his contract with the sporting goods house with which he has been connected is now at an end, but this cannot be verified."

In truth, Vardon had no intention of settling in America and looked forward to some rest and relaxation in Ganton. But he left the door open regarding his plans for a return visit. "I like the country, its people, customs, and manners," he told the *Chicago Tribune*. "I am afraid I will find England too slow after this trip. I will be back again, sooner or later, and I may come back to stay for good, the only return I could make for being treated so kindly." The champion separated his year into two distinct visits. "On my first trip, which was over a limited territory, I was not so greatly impressed with the progress golf has made here, but my second visit gave me ample

OGDEN'S CIGARETTES

H Vardon

A cigarette card issued in 1900 in England.

opportunity to observe and wonder at the popularity of the game and the skill of the players. As for myself I am feeling better and playing better than when at home."

On December 19, 1900, Vardon arrived at the dock for the steamship *Majestic,* and a reporter for the *Times* was there to document his departure. "A number of professionals gathered at the pier to bid the champion adieu, for since coming to this country Vardon has captured the open championship of the United States." He had also made a great number of friends among the American professionals.

He didn't dwell on some of the inferior courses he had played but singled out some of his favorites. "Atlantic City I consider one of the best courses in the country, and it would make an admirable site for the next amateur championship. Newport and Apawamis came close to Atlantic City in excellence." Vardon also thought Shinnecock Hills, Chicago, Midlothian, Dyker Meadow, Detroit, and Scarsdale measured up to the highest standards as well. He singled out the Adirondacks as the most beautiful area he had been to during ten months of travel encompassing nearly 100,000 miles.

The passage to England was without incident; the *Majestic* docked at Liverpool on December 26, where the London *Times* interviewed the returning champion. "Vardon said the American people had treated him most hospitably, but that the American golfers had still much to learn, as neither the players nor the links were up to mark. 'The best amateurs have a good mastery of the game, but I am frank to say that they are not yet up to the class of the leading amateurs of England and Scotland.' He intimated that he intended to return to the United States soon."

Meanwhile the champion reunited with his wife and her sister, as well as his family and soccer buddies. Brothers Tom and Alfred joined him and Jessie for a Christmas celebration, and Harry had many gifts from America to share. Harry was especially interested in the progress of Alfred, the youngest of the Vardon brothers to join the professional ranks. Alfred had found employment with the Timperley Club in Cheshire and was showing promise on the competitive circuit; some were saying he might be as good as Harry—a prediction that proved to be far from the subsequent reality.

When the Ganton football team mentioned they were a man short for the season, Vardon was more than happy to step in at goal, and the team had a very successful season. In the spring however, while diving to make a save, Vardon

Alfred Vardon followed in his brothers' footsteps, though he never achieved the same competitive notoriety.

broke a small bone in his right hand. He thought little of it at first, but it was an injury that would deteriorate along with his health in the years to come.

Vardon returned to America on two other occasions, the first more than twelve years after his maiden voyage. In 1913, he arrived with Ted Ray and played a series of matches in advance of the U.S. Open at The Country Club in Brookline. As had his tour in 1900, that encounter turned out to be a milestone in American golf history, announcing the emergence of home-grown players (in this case Francis Ouimet) who could challenge—and defeat—the dominant golfers of the world.

Vardon returned in 1920, again with Ray, and again to play exhibition matches against the best pros of the era. By then a new generation of golfers had emerged, but Vardon could still confront players such as Walter Hagen, Jock Hutchinson, Jack Burke, and Jim Barnes—even though he was twenty years past the peak of his playing powers. The 1920 U.S. Open was held at Inverness in Toledo, Ohio, and Vardon, making his final appearance in the championship, was paired with eighteen-year-old Bobby Jones, who was making his first.

Vardon's swing was the model for the cover artwork on Burnham Hare's 1914 instructional volume.

Vardon was fifty years old, but his scores proved he was still competitive, and he arrived at the first tee on the final day with the lead. He added to his margin throughout the front nine, and as he stood on the twelfth tee he enjoyed a five-stroke lead. Suddenly the light summer breeze became a gale, with wind and rain coming off distant Lake Erie raking the course. Playing into the teeth of the wind, Vardon had trouble reaching greens in regulation, and when he did, he had difficulty steadying his hands on the putter. He dropped a shot on twelve, another on thirteen. On seventeen he plunked a shot in the water, leading to a double bogey as the rain came sideways. "I was tired; my strength left me at the twelfth," he said afterward. Vardon lost seven strokes in the last seven holes, and Ray won the tournament by a single stroke. American sportswriter O. B. Keeler observed that "Fate and nothing else beat Harry Vardon that day."

The truth is, it wasn't just fate that contributed to the collapse. Vardon's demise had begun in 1903, when he was diagnosed with tuberculosis. Doctors of the day had little idea what caused the respiratory illness, but the treatment involved confinement to bed, no activity for weeks, and plenty of clean air and water. Vardon spent three months at the Mundesley Sanatorium in Norfolk, a Victorian home for wealthy patients of the disease. Initially he was allowed only two hours of stimulation a day, the remainder of the time being spent in a dark room under the bed covers. Slowly he improved, though his hands, especially the right one with the bone broken in a soccer game, were never again strong and solid. When stressed from fatigue or chilled by the cold, they shook, and putting, the one weakness in Vardon's game even when he was at his best, was negatively affected for the rest of his career. It didn't stop him from winning three more Open Championships (1903, 1911, and 1914)—but without the medical problems, and the suspension of the British tourney for five years during World War I, he undoubtedly would have won even more.

Many have written that Vardon's 1900 tour of America ignited an upswing of golf participation in the United States, but the figures do not actually bear that out. The golf boom of 1895 to 1900 was already in full swing when he arrived. Thousands of people were taking up the game, and hundreds of courses already were being built. What his visit did was demonstrate how the game could be played with the most advanced equipment and technique. No one had driven the ball as far as Vardon, and as consistently in the fairway. Few had command of their approach shots or greenside play as he did. Vardon showed that low scoring was possible, and as larger-headed clubs of better materials and the new rubber-core balls were put in the hands of amateurs, a better level of play resulted. More than anything, Vardon gave players confidence in their games and the tools to improve. Those gifts would bear fruit in American golf for decades.

Schedule of Matches

Arrived New York February 4, 1900

1. Feb. 12, 1900   Laurence Harbor CC   Perth Amboy, NJ
   Morning: M. M. Singer & John M. Ward
   Afternoon: M. M. Singer & N. C. Villepaigue
   Vardon won 11 and 10

2. Feb. 17, 1900   St. Augustine CC   St. Augustine, FL
   Willie Smith (George Low as caddie)
   Vardon won 2 and 1

3. Feb. 20, 1900   Hotel Ormond CC   Ormond Beach, FL
   Bernard Nicholls
   Vardon lost 6 and 5

4. Feb. 22, 1900   Palm Beach CC   Palm Beach, FL
   Alex Findlay
   Vardon won 1 up

5. Feb. 23, 1900   Palm Beach CC   Palm Beach, FL
   Arthur Fenn
   Vardon won 6 and 5

6. Feb. 24, 1900   Miami Beach CC   Miami Beach, FL
   George Low
   Vardon won 5 and 3

7. Mar. 2, 1900   Bon Air Hotel   Augusta, GA
   (later Augusta CC)
   Messrs. Cumming, Waller, and Denny
   Vardon won 6 and 5

8. Mar. 7, 1900   Palmetto Club   Aiken, SC
   Morning: Jones & Jimmy Mackrell
   Vardon won 1 up (18 holes)
   Afternoon: Herbert Leeds & H. R. Johnstone
   Vardon won 9 and 8 (18 holes)

9. Mar. 9, 1900   Pinehurst CC   Pinehurst, NC
   John Dunn Tucker & Lloyd Hallock
   Vardon won 8 and 7

10. Mar. 10, 1900   Pinehurst CC   Pinehurst, NC
                      George Dutton & Lathrop Baldwin
                      Vardon won 12 and 11

11. Mar. 31, 1900   Hampton Roads G&CC   Old Point Comfort, VA
                      Willie Dunn
                      Vardon won 11 and 10

12. Apr. 2, 1900   Atlantic City CC   Atlantic City, NJ
                      John Reid (pro)
                      Vardon won 76 to 95 (18 holes)

13. Apr. 3, 1900   Atlantic City CC   Atlantic City, NJ
                      Herbert Harriman & Findlay Douglas
                      Vardon won 9 and 8

14. Apr. 7, 1900   New Haven CC   New Haven, CT
                      T. M. Robertson & F. L. Myers
                      Vardon lost 3 up (18 holes)

15. Apr. 8, 1900   New Haven CC   New Haven, CT
                      Morning: A. T. Dwight Jr. & L. P. Myers
                      Vardon won 8 up (18 holes)
                      Afternoon: Charles Hitchcock Jr. & E. M. Byers
                      Vardon won 1 up (18 holes)

16. Apr. 10, 1900   Scarsdale CC   Scarsdale, NY
                      Willie Dunn
                      Vardon won 12 and 10

17. Apr. 18, 1900   Wollaston CC   Wollaston, MA
                      Morning: Arthur Fenn & Robert Stronner
                      Vardon won 4 up (18 holes)
                      Afternoon: Alex Campbell & M. C. F. Bremer
                      Vardon won 1 up (18 holes)

18. Apr. 21, 1900   Philadelphia CC   Philadelphia, PA
                      Harry Gullane & Willie Thompson
                      Vardon won 1-up

19. Apr. 24, 1900   Oakland GC   Bayside, NY
                      Walter Travis & James Douglas
                      Vardon won 6 and 5

20. Apr. 28, 1900   Allegheny CC   Pittsburgh, PA
                      Alex Findlay
                      Vardon won 11 and 10

21. May 2, 1900   Dyker Meadow GC   Brooklyn, NY
                   George Low
                   Vardon won 10 and 9

22. May 3, 1900   Wannamoissett GC   Providence, RI
                   Morning: W. D. Brownell & D. J. Sully
                   Vardon won 8 up (18 holes)
                   Afternoon: W. D. Brownell & C. L. Bremer
                   Vardon lost 2 up (18 holes)

Vardon returned to the United Kingdom for Open Championship
                   Finished second to Taylor by 8 strokes

23. July 3, 1900   Shinnecock Hills GC   Southampton, NY
                   Tom Hutchinson
                   Vardon won 12 and 11

24. July 7, 1900   Cincinnati GC   Cincinnati, OH
                   Morning: Robert White
                   Vardon won 3 up (18 holes)
                   Afternoon: Nicholas Longworth &
                      Spotwood D. Bowers
                   Vardon won 3 up (18 holes)

25. July 10, 1900 Midlothian CC   Chicago, IL
                   David Bell & Harry Turpie
                   Vardon lost 6 and 5

26. July 11, 1900 Midlothian CC   Chicago, IL
                   Vardon & Fred Herd (alternate shot)
                   Will Smith & David Bell
                   Vardon & Herd lost 3 and 2

27. July 12, 1900 Midlothian CC   Chicago, IL
                   Will Smith
                   Vardon won 4 and 2

28. July 14, 1900 Lake Geneva CC   Williams Bay, WI
                   Walter Egan & A. C. Tollifson
                   Vardon lost 1 down

29. July 18, 1900 Kenosha CC   Kenosha, WI
                   Morning: William Still & Dr. G. H. Ripley
                   Afternoon: C. C. Allen & G. A. Yule
                   Vardon lost 4 and 3

30. July 20, 1900   Chicago Golf Club   Wheaton, IL
                     James Foulis & Fred Herd
                     Vardon lost 6 and 4

31. July 21, 1900   Chicago Golf Club   Wheaton, IL
                     Will Smith
                     Vardon won 2 and 1

32. July 23, 1900   Glen View Club   Chicago
                     Lawrence Auchterlonie
                     Vardon won 3 and 2

33. July 26, 1900   CC of Detroit   Grosse Pointe, MI
                     W. H. "Bert" Way
                     Vardon won 8 and 7

34. July 28, 1900   Cleveland Golf Club   Glenville, OH
                     Joe Mitchell & Sterling Beckwith
                     Vardon won 4 and 3

35. Aug. 1, 1900   Eagle's Nest CC   Blue Mt. Lake, NY
                     Vardon played with George Armstrong
                     Harry Roy Sweney & Mortimer Singer
                     Vardon and Armstrong won

36. Aug. 2, 1900   Eagle's Nest CC   Blue Mt. Lake, NY
                     George Armstrong & Mortimer Singer
                     Vardon won 22 up

37. Aug. 6, 1900   Eagle's Nest CC   Blue Mt. Lake, NY
                     Stuart Gillespie & Harry Roy Sweney
                     Vardon won 19 up

38. Aug. 7, 1900   Eagle's Nest CC   Blue Mt. Lake, NY
                     Oscar Bunn & George Stevens
                     Vardon won 12 up (18 holes)

39. Aug. 11, 1900   Portland CC   Portland, ME
                     Alex Findlay
                     Vardon won 6 and 4

40. Aug. 13, 1900   Poland Spring Inn   Poland Spring, ME
                     Arthur Fenn
                     Vardon won 7 and 6

41. Aug. 14, 1900   Poland Spring Inn   Poland Spring, ME
                     Arthur Fenn & Alex Findlay
                     Vardon lost 2 and 1

42. Aug. 16, 1900   Mount Pleasant   Bretton Woods, NH
                     Alex Findlay & Charles Thom
                     Vardon won 5 and 4

43. Aug. 18, 1900   Maplewood   Bethlehem, NH
                     Alex and David Findlay
                     Vardon lost 2 and 1

44. Aug. 21, 1900   Waumbek GC   Jefferson, NH
                     Horace Rawlins & Alex Findlay
                     Vardon lost 4 and 3

45. Aug. 23, 1900   Profile House   Franconia, NH
                     Alex Findlay
                     Vardon won 11 and 10

46. Aug. 25, 1900   Poland Spring Inn   Poland Spring, ME
                     Arthur Fenn & Alex Findlay
                     Vardon won 4 and 2

47. Aug .27, 1900   Kebo Valley Club   Bar Harbor, ME
                     Herbert Jaques & George O. Thacher
                     Vardon won 6 and 5

48. Aug. 28, 1900   Kebo Valley Club   Bar Harbor, ME
                     George O. Thacher & James Douglas
                     Vardon won 8 and 7

49. Aug. 31, 1900   Allston GC   Boston, MA
                     Alex Findlay
                     Vardon won 5 and 4

50. Sept. 2, 1900   Newport CC   Newport, RI
                     Morning: R. C. Watson Jr. & Charles Hitchcock Jr.
                     Vardon won 2 up (18 holes)
                     Afternoon: Alex Findlay & Robert Stronner
                     Vardon lost 4 and 2 (18 holes)

51. Sept. 4, 1900   Seapuit Links   Osterville, MA
                     Alex Findlay
                     Vardon won 79 to 81 (18 holes)

52. Sept. 8, 1900   Seabright GC   Seabright, NJ
                     Willie Norton & F. W. Menzies
                     Vardon lost 1 up

53. Sept. 11, 1900   Essex County Club   Manchester, MA
                     Joseph Lloyd
                     Vardon won

54. Sept. 12, 1900   Essex County Club   Manchester, MA
                      Joseph Lloyd & Jack Dingwall
                      Vardon won 1 up

55. Sept. 15, 1900   Richmond County CC   Staten Island, NY
                      Morning: Douglas Bonner & C. T. Stout
                      Vardon won 5 up (18 holes)
                      Afternoon: John R. Chadwick & Albert E. Paterson
                      Vardon won 7 up (18 holes)

56. Sept. 18, 1900   Hartford GC   Hartford, CT
                      (Tom Bendelow as caddie and partner in
                         practice match)
                      Morning: William Watson & James H. T. Brown
                      Vardon won 3 and 2 (18 holes)
                      Afternoon: Ralph W. Cutter & Frank R. Cooley
                      Vardon won 3 and 2 (18 holes)

57. Sept. 19, 1900   Morris County CC   Morristown, NJ
                      Morning: James A. Tyng & John G. Bates
                      Vardon won 4 and 2 (18 holes)
                      Afternoon: Played with Leland Garretson vs. same
                      Vardon won 3 and 2 (18 holes)

58. Sept. 20, 1900   Morris County CC   Morristown, NJ
                      George Low & Tom Hutchinson
                      Vardon lost 8 and 7

59. Sept. 22, 1900   Rosedale Greens   Toronto, Canada
                      George Lyon & Vere Brown
                      Vardon won 5 and 4

60. Sept. 25, 1900   Royal Montreal (Dixie)   Montreal, Canada
                      Morning: George Cumming & Tom Smith
                      Vardon lost 1 down (18 holes)
                      Afternoon: Percy Taylor & Gordon Macdougall
                      Vardon won 5 and 4 (18 holes)

61. Oct. 4, 1900   Chicago GC (U.S. Open)   Wheaton, IL
                      Vardon won by 2 over J. H. Taylor

62. Oct. 9, 1900   CC of Scranton   Scranton, PA
                      Morning: A. Z. Huntington & Thomas H. Watkins
                      Vardon won 2 and 1
                      Afternoon: J. H. Brooks & T. C. Fuller
                      Vardon won 2 and 1

63. Oct. 12, 1900   Brae Burn GC   Newton, MA
                     Bernard Nicholls
                     Vardon lost 1 down

64. Oct. 16, 1900   Oakley CC   Watertown, MA
                     Alex Findlay & Donald Ross
                     Vardon won 6 and 5

65. Oct. 18, 1900   Merrimack Valley CC   Lawrence, MA
                     Alex Findlay
                     Vardon won 1 up (37 holes)

66. Oct. 20, 1900   Fall River CC   Fall River, MA
                     Vardon played with R. M. Hawkins
                     Arthur Fenn & Alex Findlay
                     Vardon won 3 and 2

67. Oct. 23, 1900   Hawthorne GC   New Bedford, MA
                     Alex Findlay
                     Vardon won 7 and 6

68. Oct. 24, 1900   Vesper CC   Tyngsborough, MA
                     Alex Findlay
                     Vardon won 13 and 12

69. Oct. 25, 1900   Vesper CC   Tyngsborough, MA
                     Jack Harland
                     Vardon won 6 and 5

70. Oct. 26, 1900   Albany CC   Albany, NY
                     Harry Roy Sweney
                     Vardon won 9 up (18 holes)

71. Oct. 27, 1900   Albany CC   Albany, NY
                     Morning: John Reid Jr. & George Pierson
                     Afternoon: John Reid Jr. & Valentine Fitzjohn
                     Vardon won 4 and 3

72. Nov. 3, 1900   Chevy Chase Club   Chevy Chase, MD
                     Willie Tucker & Donald Ball
                     Vardon won 6 and 5

73. Nov. 6, 1900   Fairfield County CC   Greenwich, CT
                     Findlay Douglas
                     Vardon won 10 and 8

74. Nov. 10, 1900   Apawamis CC   Rye, NY
                     Willie Davis & Maturin Ballou
                     Vardon won 7 and 6

75. Nov. 18, 1900   Van Cortlandt Park   New York, NY
                     Morning: Val Flood & William Freeland
                     Vardon won 5 and 4 (18 holes)
                     Afternoon: Val Flood & William C. Morrill
                     Vardon won 7 and 6 (18 holes)

76. Nov. 24, 1900   Chevy Chase Club   Chevy Chase, MD
                     Willie Tucker & Donald Ball
                     Vardon won 1 up

77. Dec. 7, 1900   Overland Park GC   Denver, CO
                     Walter Fairbanks (received half a stroke per hole)
                     Vardon lost 4 and 3

78. Dec. 9, 1900   Overland Park GC   Denver, CO
                     Walter Fairbanks, James Russell &
                       Frank L. Woodard
                     Vardon won 3 and 2

79. Dec. 10, 1900   Town and Gown   Colorado Springs, CO
                     Morning: W. W. Campbell & H. B. Davis
                     Vardon won 3 and 2
                     Afternoon: W. K. Jewett & H. B. Davis
                     Vardon won 1 up

Departed for the United Kingdom December 19, 1900

Acknowledgments

Some unsolicited advice to authors: When you undertake a project such as this, start a list on day one of the people who have helped. That way, in the final hours before the manuscript goes off to the publisher, you're not struggling to remember everyone who lent an ear or assistance for the past two years.

First and foremost on this list is my co-author Brian Siplo. Brian's enthusiasm for the subject and compulsiveness to uncover every detail have helped to drive this endeavor since its launch. Searching his extensive resources, he has uncovered names and places that needed to be fleshed out, and he picked up various trails when I have grown frustrated with an apparent dead end. In addition he has placed Vardon in his historical context, educating me on British golf during the period and how Vardon fit in. He has provided a wealth of images, shared memorabilia from his collection, and edited every word of the manuscript for historical accuracy and flow.

Brian also contacted every club that Vardon visited—at least the ones that still exist—to see if anything personal, anecdotal, or physical relating to the visit resides in their clubhouse. Although the search turned up very little, we thank the clubs that took the time to respond to our queries and search for memorabilia and information.

Patrick White of Meadow Ridge Media has edited the book for language, usage, context, and flow, as well as listening endlessly to my excitement over boring details and outrageous anecdotes. Bouncing ideas back and forth with Pat has greatly enhanced my writing for the past decade. The genesis of this project dates from 2001, when, as editor of the *New Hampshire Golf* magazine, I assigned an article about Vardon in New Hampshire to Peter Georgiady. His fine article stimulated my interest in the entire tour; thanks, Pete.

Many thanks also to Alastair Johnston who opened his amazing library to my research requests. Many of the images in this book would never have been retrieved without his generosity.

We'd also like to acknowledge the help and assistance of Allan Wallach, Frank Nicholls, David Cornwell, Kevin Mendik, Charlie Tadge, Audrey Moriarty and the Tufts Archives, Bob Montgomery, Rob Halpert, Bruce Wood, Howard Schickler, Dick Donovan, Nancy

Greenlee, Tony Pioppi, Randy Jensen, Rudy Zocchi, Ed Homsey, J. Peter Martin, Pat Kennedy, Matt Dodds, Pete Trenham, Stuart Bendelow, Jim Apfelbaum, Andrew Crewe, Craig Ammerman, Rand Jerris, Doug Stark, and all the people at the USGA, but especially Patty Moran. I also appreciate the willingness of Ann Arbor Media Group to publish the book and the assistance of Lynne Johnson, Carol Bokas, and everyone else at Ann Arbor Media Group.

This book would not have been possible without the firsthand accounts written by the reporters from the *New York Times, Boston Globe, Chicago Tribune,* and the other major papers that followed Vardon around the country to detail his exploits. And many of those reports would have been lost to history had it not been for ProQuest and their amazing system of retrieval that has brought the written word of 1900 to light in today's world. Many writers appreciate all the work they have done to digitize old newspapers.

No one can devote as much time as a project like this takes without the support of their family. Although they probably don't understand what drives me to work until 11 P.M. down at my office when I should be home having dinner and taking care of home projects, they haven't kicked me out yet, and for that I thank my wife Kathie Hickman, my son Griffin, and my daughter Simone. I hope my children feel as passionate and fulfilled by their eventual career choices as I have been fortunate to be about mine.

Bibliography

Apawamis Club. *Fifty Years of Apawamis 1890–1940,* New York, 1940.

Batten, Jack. *Rosedale Golf Club: The First 100 Years,* Toronto, 1993.

Barclay, James A. *Golf in Canada,* Toronto: McClelland & Stewart, Inc., 1992.

Beckwith, J. P. *East Coast of Florida,* 1901.

Bendelow, Stuart W. *Thomas "Tom" Bendelow,* Georgia: Williams and Co., 2006.

Brae Burn. *Fifty Years of Brae Burn, 1897–1947,* Massachusetts, 1947.

Buckley, Edmund. *The History of Fall River Country Club,* Massachusetts, 1990.

Byrdy, Stan. *Augusta and Aiken in Golf's Golden Age,* South Carolina: Arcadia, 2002.

Campbell, Duncan C. *The Royal Montreal Golf Club, 1873–1973,* Montreal, 1973.

Caner, George C., Jr. *History of the Essex County Club, 1893–1993,* Massachusetts, 1995.

The Cincinnati Country Club. *1895–1944 Club Handbook,* 1944.

Cooper, J. M. *Early United States Golf Clubs.*

Cornish, Geoffrey S., and Ronald E. Whitten. *The Architects of Golf,* New York: HarperCollins, 1993.

Country Club of Detroit. *In Good Company,* Detroit, 1997.

Dahill, Edwin M., Jr. *The Hartford Golf Club, 1896–1996,* Connecticut, 1995.

Dutchess County Historical Society. *Yearbook,* Volume 83: 2001–2002, New York, 2003.

Elliott, Len, and Barbara Kelly. *Who's Who in Golf,* New York: Arlington House, 1976.

Evans, Alun. *The Golf Majors Records & Yearbook,* London: Brassey's Sports, 1998.

Frisbie, Louis K. *Florida's Fabled Inns,* Florida: Imperial Publishing, 1980.

Georgiady, Peter. *North American Club Makers,* North Carolina: Airlie Hall, 1998.

Golfers Magazine. "The Grip in Golf," Chicago, 1922.

Goodner, Ross. *Chicago Golf Club, 1892–1992,* Chicago, 1991.

Govedarica, Tom. *Chicago Golf: The First 100 Years,* Chicago: Eagle Communications Group, 1991.

Graffis, Herb. *The PGA,* New York: Thomas Y. Crowell Co., 1975.

Harber, Paul F. *The Complete Guide to Golf on Cape Cod, Nantucket & Martha's Vineyard,* Massachusetts: Peninsula Press, 1993.

Howell, Audrey. *Harry Vardon,* London: Stanley Paul, 1991.

Jackson, Alan F. *The British Professional Golfers 1887–1930: A Register,* Worcestershire: Grant Books, 1994.

James Carter & Co. *The Practical Greenkeeper,* London, 1901.

Johnston, Alastair. *Vardon to Woods,* Cleveland, 1999.

Kebo Valley Club. *The Spirit of Kebo, 1888–1988,* Maine, 1988.

Kebo Valley Club. *Sixtieth Anniversary Year, 1888–1948,* Maine, 1948.

Kelly, William E. *Birth of the Birdie,* New Jersey: Atlantic City CC, 1997.

Kerr, W. A. R. *Golf in Canada,* Toronto: The Canadian Magazine, August 1901.

Klein, Bradley S. *Discovering Donald Ross,* Michigan: Sleeping Bear Press, 2001.

Leahey, Brendan D. *One Hundred Years at Vesper,* Massachusetts, 1979.

Machat, Udo. *The Golf Ball Book,* California: Sport Images, 2000.

Magowan, David. *Scarsdale Golf Club Inc., 1898–1948,* New York, 1948.

Martin, H. B. *Fifty Years of American Golf,* New York, 1936.

Martin, J. Peter. *Adirondack Golf Courses … Past and Present,* New York: North Country Books, 1987.

McMahon, Terrance A. *Country Club of Scranton, 1896–1987,* Pennsylvania, 1987.

Metropolitan Golf Association with Dr. William L. Quirin. *Golf Clubs of the MGA,* New York: Golf Magazine, 1997.

Moriarty, Audrey. *Pinehurst: Golf, History, and the Good Life,* Michigan: Sports Media Group, 2005.

Newman, Josiah (editor). *1900 Official Golf Guide,* New York.

Oakley Country Club. *Notes on a Happy Half-Century,* Massachusetts, 1948.

Odermatt, Richard W. *New Haven Country Club, 1898–1998,* Connecticut, 1998.

Palmetto Golf Club. *The First 100 Years,* Virginia: Donning Co., 1992.

Paulhus, Don. *Wannamoisett Country Club,* Rhode Island, 1998.

Peper, George. *Shinnecock Hills Golf Club, 1891–1991,* New York, 1991.

Philadelphia Country Club. *The History, 1890–1965,* Pennsylvania, 1965.

Quirin, William L. *Morris County Golf Club, 1894–1994,* Virginia: Donning Co., 1995.

Quirin, William L. *The Greenwich Country Club, 1892–1992,* Virginia: Donning Company, 1993.

Seagrave, Alice D. *Golf Retold: The Story of Golf in Cleveland,* Cleveland: Cleveland Women's Golf Association, 1940.

Shapiro, Mel. *Golf: A Turn of the Century Treasury,* New Jersey: Castle, 1986.

Spatz, Richard E. *The History of Allegheny Country Club,* Pennsylvania, 1995.

USGA Record Book, 1895–1971, New Jersey: USGA, 1972.

Vardon, Harry. *My Golfing Life,* London: Hutchinson & Co., 1933.

Vardon, Harry. *The Complete Golfer,* New York: Doubleday, Page & Co., 1922.

Wexler, Daniel. *The Book of Golfers,* Michigan: Sports Media Group, 2005.

White Bear Yacht Club. *Reflections, 1889–1989,* Minnesota, 1989.

Wollaston Golf Club. *The Story of an Old Club, 1895–1945,* Massachusetts, 1945.

Wood, John. *The Cincinnati Country Club: A History,* Ohio, 1991.

Extensive use of the following newspapers and periodicals:

American Golfer
Among the Clouds
Atlanta Constitution
Boston Evening Transcript
Boston Globe
Chicago Tribune
Country Life
Fall River Daily Herald
Golf Illustrated (British)
Golf/USGA Bulletin
The Golfer
Harper's Official Golf Guide
Hartford Courant
The Hill-Top
London Times
Los Angeles Times
Mainly About People
Manchester Guardian
New York Commercial Advertiser
New York Sun
New York Times
Outing
Pinehurst Outlook
Portland Telegram
Spalding Golf Guide
Washington Post
White Mountain Echo

Index

Illustrative material is shown in italics.

Vardon, Harry *(continued)*
tournaments
  early tournament play 19–20
  Open Championship wins 1,
    2, 16, 20, 21, 27, 180. *See
    also* Open Championship,
    1900
  See also U.S. Open, 1900;
    1913; 1920
  and training 20, 88
  on visiting America 1, 3–4, 173
  wife of. *See* Vardon, Jessie
    Bryant
Vardon, Jessie Bryant 5, 6, 19,
    87–88, 178, 179
Vardon, Philip 15–16, 18
Vardon, Tom 16, 18, 19, 20, 21, *21,*
    178–79
Vardon Flyer 4, 7–8
Vesper Country Club 160–61, *161,*
    173, 189
Villepique, N.C. 11, 183

Walker, George 98
Wall, Tom 144
Wannamoisett Country Club
    83–85, *84, 85,* 87, 185
Ward, John M. 11, 183
Washington Golf Club 164, 168
Washington Park Club 97, 101
Watkins, Thomas H. 151

Watson, R. C., Jr. 87, 129, *129*
Watson, William 138
Waumbek Golf Club *122,* 123–24,
    130, 158, 187
Way, W. H. "Bert" 106–7
Westbrook 129
Western Golf Association 103
White, Jack 27
White, Robert 91, 93, *93,* 94
White Bear Yacht Club 21
Williams, Elmer 98
Wilmington Country Club 63
Wilson, R. B. 130
Wilson, Robert 157
Winton, James 120
Wollaston Golf Club 72, 74, 184
Woodard, Frank L. 175
Woods, Tiger 31
Woodstock Country Club 171
Woodway 25
Workingman's Club 18
Wright, George 72, 127
Wright and Ditson Sporting Goods
    4, 71. *See also* Spalding
    Company
Wykagyl 124
Wylie, W. Gill 131

Yale University, golf team 66–69,
    131
Yule, George A. 100